Cake Mix Cookies

Also by Camilla V. Saulsbury

Cookie Dough Delights

Brownie Mix Bliss

No-Bake Cookies

Puff Pastry Perfection

Panna Cotta

Cake Mix Cookies

More Than 175 Delectable Cookie Recipes
That Begin with a Box of Cake Mix

Camilla V. Saulsbury

CUMBERLAND HOUSE
NASHVILLE, TN

CAKE MIX COOKIES
PUBLISHED BY CUMBERLAND HOUSE PUBLISHING, INC.
431 Harding Industrial Drive
Nashville, TN 37211

Cover design: JulesRulesDesign
Text design: Lisa Taylor

Library of Congress Cataloging-in-Publication Data

Saulsbury, Camilla V.
  Cake Mix Cookies : more than 175 delectable recipes that begin with a box of cake mix / by Camilla V. Saulsbury.
    p. cm.
  Includes bibliographical references and index.
  ISBN 1-58182-475-0 (pbk. : alk. paper)
1. Cookies. I. Title.
  TX772.S2578 2005
  641.8'654—dc22

2005016069

Printed in Canada
3 4 5 6 7 8 9 — 12 11 10 09 08 07

To Becca & Sean

Contents

Acknowledgments

To Kevin, for his patience and love. To my publisher, Ron Pitkin, for his enthusiasm, support, and guidance with this and all of my cookbook projects. To Julia Pitkin, for her great style and taste in the design of this and all of my books. To Lisa Taylor— how lucky I am to have such a brilliant editor. To the entire staff of Cumberland House Publishing, who have worked tirelessly behind the scenes to make this book happen. To Jane, Brian, Bernice, and Holly, for giving me flexibility in finishing my dissertation project while simultaneously writing this book. And to my parents, Dan and Charlotte, for inspiring me in all of my creative endeavors.

Cake Mix Cookies

Introduction

It's always a good time to rediscover the age-old comfort of cookies. Try conjuring an image more comforting than a kitchen warm with the smells of sweet vanilla, fragrant cinnamon, and fresh butter; on the kitchen counter, a cooling rack piled high with fresh-from-the-oven delights studded with chocolate chips and crunchy pecans. It is a cause for celebration in itself—particularly when the cookie recipe is as quick and convenient as opening a box of cake mix.

That's right—cake mix. A standard 18.25-ounce box of cake mix is the secret to simple and successful cookie baking. Even better, the results are assuredly irresistible. A box of cake mix can give home bakers the same head start for baking cookies as for baking cakes. Moreover, cake mix simplifies steps and offers insurance (in the form of accurately premeasured and mixed flour, sugar, and leavening) that the time spent baking will lead to sweet success time and again. With a few extra ingredients, turns of the spoon, and whirs of the mixer, cake mix can make any home baker a prize cookie baker.

And oh, what cookies to choose from! You may have seen a handful of cake mix cookie recipes here and there, but never a collection as extensive as this. Turn the pages and you'll find an enticing array of drop, shaped, filled, and bar cookie options that are scrumptious, satisfying, simple to make, and pretty to serve.

Quite a few all-American favorites are starting points throughout the book—Blue-Ribbon Chocolate-Chip, Chewy Oatmeal Raisin, Jam Thumbprints, and Dark Chocolate Brownies are but a few. New takes on classic European cookies are also well-represented—for example, crunchy Italian biscotti, tender French madeleines, and rich Viennese teacakes.

Finally, a hearty helping of serendipity is stirred up to create a host of new cookie options guaranteed to tempt one and all; they are destined to become new classics. How about Gooey Triple-Chocolate Chess Squares for your next birthday party? Or

Blackberry-Lemon Buttermilk Bars for a summer cookout at the park? Or perhaps a holiday cookie plate filled to overflowing with Chocolate Blackout Cookies, Dulce de Leche Crisps, Fresh Pear Cookies with Browned Butter Icing, and Sesame Honey Crinkles? This is the stuff of which sweet dreams are made.

Once the cake mix cookie baking commences, one thing will be immediately self-evident: each and every cookie in this book will lead home bakers—and the lucky recipients of their efforts—straight to the comfort zone. So why wait? Don an apron, experiment, and have fun. Be it ever so humble, there's no taste like a homemade cookie.

Smart Cookie Tips

• Read the recipe thoroughly. Note the required ingredients, equipment needed as well as the chilling, baking, and cooling times.

• Gather the necessary ingredients, checking for freshness (see the "Cake Mix Cookie Panty" section that follows for tips on how to do so).

• Gather the necessary equipment, including oven mitts and cooling racks.

• Prep the ingredients as needed, such as chopping nuts, zesting lemons, softening cream cheese, or melting butter.

• Prepare any baking pans or cookie sheets as specified in the recipe. If no advanced preparation is needed, set the pan or sheet aside so that it is ready to be used when needed.

• Reread the recipe.

• Preheat the oven. Turn the oven to the specified temperature for 10–15 minutes prior to baking to give the oven adequate time to heat up to the correct temperature.

• Use an oven thermometer. Indispensable, inexpensive (under $5), and readily available in the baking sections of most supermarkets or at any kitchen supply store, these handy devices allow you to check the accuracy and consistency of your oven temperature. Oven temperatures tend to be too high or too low; armed with the correct information from your thermometer, you can adjust accordingly.

• Precisely measure all of the ingredients. Baking is a science, hence small variations can have a significant effect on the final product. See the "Measuring Ingredients" section for tips on measuring dry, liquid, and moist ingredients.

• Mix ingredients according to recipe specifications.

• Use a kitchen timer. This allows for precision and helps ensure the end product is not overcooked. One or 2 minutes can make a world of difference in cookie baking so ensure your results with a reliable timer.

• Check the baked good at the earliest time specified. For example, if a recipe reads "Bake for 30–35 minutes until toothpick inserted near the center comes clean," then check for doneness at 30 minutes. Continue baking if needed and continue checking every 1 minute.

The Cake Mix Cookie Pantry

Cake Mixes: All of the recipes in this book were tested using an 18.25-ounce box of cake mix. These included, for example, name brand mixes such as Betty Crocker®, Duncan Hines®, and Pillsbury® cake mixes, as well as store brand mixes such as Kroger® and Safeway® brands. Flavors vary slightly by manufacturer, so take note if you prefer one brand over another.

Cake mixes contain flour, sugar, leavening (baking powder and baking soda), fat, salt flavoring and coloring in precise, premeasured proportion. They have a one-year shelf life, so it is a great idea to stock up, particularly when cake mixes are on sale (which is often). For spur-of-the-moment cookie baking, try keeping one or two each of chocolate, yellow, lemon, white, and spice cake mixes in the pantry.

Butter: Butter is used in many of the recipes throughout the book to bolster the flavor of the cookies, brownies, or bars. Either unsalted or lightly salted butter may be used where butter is listed as an ingredient in this book.

Butter freshness: Fresh butter should have a delicate cream flavor and pale yellow color. Butter quickly picks up off-flavors during storage and when exposed to oxygen; once the carton is opened, place it in a resealable plastic storage bag or airtight container. Store it away from foods with strong odors, especially items such as onions or garlic.

Avoid using butter to coat baking pans and sheets. Because butter melts at a lower temperature than other "greasing" ingredients, such as vegetable shortening, it may leave ungreased gaps on sheets and pans, causing baked goods to stick. Second, butter can burn, particularly when baking above 350°. At best, what you're baking will be overly brown; at worst, scorched.

Melting butter: Melted butter is used in many recipes throughout this book. For best results, cut the specified amount of butter into small pieces, place in a small saucepan, and allow to melt over the lowest heat setting of the burner. Once the butter has melted, remove pan from heat and cool. To speed the cooling pour the melted butter into a small bowl or liquid measuring cup.

Softening butter: Softened butter is also required in several recipes throughout the book. The traditional method for softening butter is to remove the needed amount from the refrigerator and let it stand 30–45 minutes at room temperature. Cutting the butter into small chunks will reduce the softening time to about 15 minutes. If time is really limited, try grating the cold butter on the large holes of a cheese grater. The small bits of butter will be soft in just a few minutes. Alternatively, place the cold butter between sheets of waxed paper and hit it several times with a rolling pin. Avoid softening butter in the microwave. It will typically melt at least part of the butter, even if watched closely.

Chocolate: Two general types of chocolate are used throughout this book. The first type is chocolate chips, available in semisweet, milk, white, and miniature semisweet. Some premium brands offer bittersweet chocolate chips, which may be used interchangeably with semisweet chocolate chips. The second general type of chocolate is baking chocolate, which is typically available in 6- or 8-ounce packages with the chocolate most often individually wrapped in 1-ounce squares or occasionally in 2-ounce bars. It is available in unsweetened, bittersweet, semisweet, milk, and white chocolate varieties.

Chocolate storage: Store both chocolate chips and baking chocolate in a dry, cool place between 60° and 78°. Wrapping chocolate in moisture-proof wrap or in a ziplock plastic bag is a good idea if the temperature is higher or the humidity is above 50 percent. Chocolate can also be stored in the fridge, but let it stand at room temperature before using.

Blooming chocolate: If the chocolate from your pantry has a white, crusty-looking film on it, don't toss it. This is commonly called "bloom" and develops when the chocolate is exposed to varying temperatures, from hot to cold. The change in heat allows the cocoa butter to melt and rise to the surface of the chocolate. Bloom does not affect the quality or flavor of the chocolate. The chocolate will look normal again once it is melted or used in baking.

Cream Cheese: All of the recipes in this book use "brick"-style cream cheese, which is typically packaged in 3-ounce and 8-ounce rectangular packages. For best results avoid using soft-spread, flavored, or whipped cream cheese.

To soften cream cheese, unwrap it and cut it into chunks with a sharp knife. Let it stand at room temperature 30–45 minutes until softened. For speed softening, place the chunks of cream cheese on a microwavable plate or in a microwavable bowl and microwave on high for 15 seconds. If necessary, microwave 5 or 10 seconds longer.

Eggs: Use large eggs in all of the recipes in this book. Select clean, fresh eggs which have been handled properly and refrigerated. Do not use dirty, cracked, or leaking eggs that may have a bad odor or unnatural color when cracked open. They may have become contaminated with harmful bacteria such as salmonella. Cold eggs are easiest to separate; eggs at room temperature beat to high volume.

Egg freshness: Eggs may be checked for freshness by filling a deep bowl with enough cold water to cover an egg. Place the egg in the water. If the egg lies on its side on the bottom of the bowl, it is fresh. If the egg stands up and bobs on the bottom, it isn't quite as fresh, but is still acceptable for baking. If the egg floats on the surface, it should be discarded.

Margarine: Margarine may be substituted for butter, but it is not recommended because it lacks the rich flavor that butter offers. However, if using margarine in place of butter, it is essential that it is a 100 percent vegetable oil, solid stick. Margarine spreads—in tub or stick form—will alter the liquid and fat combination of the recipe, leading to either unsatisfactory or downright disastrous results. You can determine the fat percentage in one of two ways. In some cases, the percentage is printed on the box. If it reads anything less than 100 percent oil, it is a spread and should be avoided for baking purposes. If the percentage is not printed on the outside of the box, flip it over and check the calories. If it is 100 calories per tablespoon, it is 100 percent vegetable oil; any less, and it is less than 100 percent and should not be used.

Nonstick Cooking Spray: I prefer to use nonstick cooking spray, such as PAM, for "greasing" pans because of its convenience. However, solid vegetable shortening, such as Crisco, may also be used. Both are flavorless and coat pans and cookie sheets evenly.

When spraying or greasing baking pans for brownies, be sure to coat only the bottom of the pan. If the inside walls of the pan are coated, the brownies will not rise properly.

When making bars, the entire inside of the pan may be coated in cooking spray. Cookie sheets should be given only a very light spraying or greasing for best results.

Shelled nuts: Use plain, unsalted nuts unless specified otherwise in the recipe. To determine whether shelled nuts are fresh, taste them: they should taste and smell fresh, not rancid with an off-flavor. Frozen nuts are prone to freezer burn if stored improperly and may taste old or stale (old, stale, or rancid nuts will ruin the baked product). Shelled nuts should also have a crisp texture, should be relatively uniform in color, and should not be shriveled or discolored in spots.

Toasting nuts. Toasting nuts before adding them to a recipe can greatly intensify their flavor and hence their contribution to a recipe. To toast without turning on the oven, place them in an ungreased skillet over medium heat (3–4 minutes), stirring frequently, until golden brown (note that this method works best with chopped, as opposed to whole, nuts). To oven-toast, spread the nuts in a single layer in a baking pan or on a cookie sheet. Bake at 350° for 10–15 minutes, stirring occasionally, or until golden brown. Cool the nuts before adding them to the recipe.

Spices: All of the recipes in this book use ground, as opposed to whole, spices. Freshness is everything with ground spices. The best way to determine if a ground spice is fresh is to open the container and smell it. If it still has a strong fragrance, it is still acceptable for use. If not, toss it and make a new purchase.

Vanilla Extract: Vanilla extract adds a sweet, fragrant flavor to baked goods and is particularly good for enhancing the flavor of chocolate. It is produced by extracting the flavor of dried vanilla beans with an alcohol and water mixture. It is then aged for several months. The three most common types of beans used to make vanilla extract are Bourbon-Madagascar, Mexican, and Tahitian.

Store vanilla extract in a cool, dark place, with the bottle tightly closed to prevent it from evaporating and losing flavor. It will stay fresh for about two years unopened and for one year after being opened.

Imitation vanilla flavoring can be substituted for vanilla extract, but it may have a slight or prominent artificial taste depending on the brand. It is about half the cost of real vanilla extract; however, it's worth the extra expense of splurging on the real thing.

Other Extracts & Flavorings: Other extracts and flavorings, such as maple, rum, lemon and brandy, are used in recipes throughout this book. They can be found in the baking aisle alongside the vanilla extract. Store in a cool, dark place to maintain optimal flavor.

Evaporated Milk: A canned milk product that is made by evaporating milk to half of its volume, producing a creamy texture and rich taste. All of the recipes in this book that require evaporated milk were tested using regular (as opposed to lowfat) evaporated milk.

Sweetened Condensed Milk: Canned evaporated milk that has been reduced further and sweetened with sugar. Although it is available in lowfat varieties, use the regular variety for optimal results.

Measuring Ingredients

Measuring Dry Ingredients: When measuring a dry ingredient such as sugar, flour, spices, or salt, spoon it into the appropriate-size dry measuring cup or measuring spoon, heaping it up over the top. Next, slide a straight-edged utensil, such as a knife, across the top to level off the extra. Be careful not to shake or tap the cup or spoon to settle the ingredient or you will have more than you need.

Measuring Liquid Ingredients: Use a clear plastic or glass measuring cup or container with lines up the sides to measure liquid ingredients. Set the container on the counter and pour the liquid to the appropriate mark. Lower your head to read the measurement at eye level.

Measuring Moist Ingredients: Some moist ingredients, such as brown sugar, coconut, and dried fruits, must be firmly packed into the measuring cup to be measured accurately. Use a dry measuring cup for these ingredients. Fill the measuring cup to slightly overflowing, then pack down the ingredient firmly with the back of a spoon. Add more of the ingredient and pack down again until the cup is full and even with the top of the measure.

Measuring Butter: Butter is typically packaged in stick form with markings on the wrapper indicating tablespoon and cup measurements. Use a sharp knife to cut off the amount needed for a recipe.

$\frac{1}{4}$ cup = $\frac{1}{2}$ stick = 4 tablespoons = 2 ounces
$\frac{1}{2}$ cup = 1 stick = $\frac{1}{4}$ pound = 4 ounces
1 cup = 2 sticks = $\frac{1}{2}$ pound = 8 ounces
2 cups = 4 sticks = 1 pound = 16 ounces

Measuring Cream Cheese: Like sticks of butter, bricks of cream cheese are typically packaged with markings on the wrapper indicating tablespoon and cup measurements. Use a sharp knife to cut off the amount needed for a recipe.

Measuring Spices, Salt, Baking Powder, & Baking Soda: Use the standard measuring spoon size specified in the recipe and be sure the spoon is dry when measuring. Fill a standard measuring spoon to the top and level with a spatula or knife. When a recipe calls for a dash of a spice or salt, use about $\frac{1}{16}$ of a teaspoon. A pinch is considered to be the amount of salt that can be held between the tips of the thumb and forefinger and is also approximately $\frac{1}{16}$ of a teaspoon.

Measuring Nuts: Spoon nuts into a dry measuring cup to the top. Four ounces of nuts is the equivalent of 1 cup chopped nuts.

Measuring Extracts & Flavorings: Fill the standard measuring spoon size specified in the recipe to the top, being careful not to let any spill over. It's a good idea to avoid measuring extracts or flavorings over the mixing bowl because the spillover will go into the bowl and you will not know the amount of extract or flavoring you have added.

Cooling & Serving

Cooling: Cool all baked goods on cooling racks immediately following baking unless specified otherwise in the recipe.

Cookies should be transferred to cooling racks immediately following removal from the oven unless specified otherwise. A metal spatula or pancake turner is the best tool for transferring cookies to cooling racks. Many of the cookie recipes note that the cookies should be left on the cookie sheets for several minutes after baking before being transferred to cooling sheets. The heat from the pan allows the cookies to continue baking (without overbaking and drying out in the oven). Follow the directions and then transfer the cookies to cooling racks.

Bars and brownies are best cooled in the pan before cutting.

Cutting Bar Cookies: Cut cooled bars with a plastic or table knife to ensure smooth-sided bars. For precision cutting, use a pastry scraper.

To cut particularly soft or gooey bars or brownies while they are still in the pan, move the knife across the pan in an up and down sawing motion from one end to the other until they are cut. Place the pan in the freezer for 30 minutes, if needed, to make the cutting job easier.

A hot knife will also make bar cookies cut more easily: before starting, dip the sharp knife in hot water and wipe with a dry kitchen towel. When cutting gooey brownies or a similar type of bar, try not to press down with the knife or the cut edges will squish together. After each cut, clean and reheat the knife by dipping it in hot water and wiping with a paper towel before resuming.

Storage

General Storage: Store cookies and bars in an airtight container at room temperature for optimal freshness, unless specified otherwise in the recipe. Sturdier cookies and bars can be placed in a ziplock plastic bag; more delicate varieties are better off stacked between layers of waxed paper in a plastic container. Bar cookies can be stacked in a container between layers of waxed paper or stored in their baking pan. Cover the top tightly with aluminum foil, wrap, or a lid.

Freezing Already-Baked Cookies: Drop, shaped, filled, and bar cookies may be frozen for future enjoyment. Custard and cream cheese–filled bar cookies and brownies do not fare as well when frozen. If the cookies call for icing or frosting, do not add it until the cookies have been thawed at a future date. Cookies can be frosted after thawing at room temperature for 15–30 minutes.

For best results, freeze the cookies as soon as possible after they are completely cooled. Place them in freezer bags or airtight freezer containers for up to six months. Double wrap the cookies to prevent them from getting freezer burn or absorbing odors from the freezer and label the bag clearly with the name of the cookie and the date.

Equipment

Baking Pans: Using the correct-size pan specified in the recipe is critical to the success of all baking. Bars and other baked goods that are made in a too-large pan, for example, will be overbaked, and those in a too-small pan will be underbaked.

If you only have a few pans, and none are the pan size specified, a solution still exists. Use the pan size that you have. If it's larger than what is called for, use a shorter bake time. If it's smaller than what is called for, use a longer bake time and reduce the oven temperature 25 degrees.

For best results, use shiny metal pans for all of the bar recipes in this book. Not only are the bars easier to remove but metal pans allow the crusts of layered bars to become crispy. If possible, avoid using dark pans. If a dark pan is all you have, reduce the oven temperature 25 degrees as indicated in the bar recipes.

Cookie Sheets: Cookies are best baked on light-colored, dull-finished, heavy-gauge cookie sheets. Shiny sheets work best for cookies that should not brown too much on the bottom. Avoid using cookie sheets with high sides; they can deflect heat as well as make it difficult to remove the cookies for cooling. As a general rule, cookie sheets should be two inches narrower and shorter than the oven to allow for even baking.

It is best to avoid dark aluminum cookie sheets; the brown or almost black finish absorbs heat quickly, causing bottoms of cookies to overbrown or burn. If using these sheets is the only option, decrease the baking time and lower the temperature slightly (about 25 degrees).

Nonstick cookie sheets are easier to clean and help ensure even baking; however, the dough may not spread as much and you may end up with a thicker cookie. On the other hand, rich cookies can spread if baked on a greased sheet. Follow the manufacturer's instructions if using a cookie sheet with a nonstick coating; the oven temperature may need to be reduced by 25 degrees.

Also follow the manufacturer's instructions if using insulated cookie sheets, which are made from two sheets of metal with a layer of air between for insulation. Cookies will not brown as much on the bottom, so it may be hard to tell when the cookies are done. Also, cookies may take slightly longer to bake.

Aluminum Foil (Foil-Lining Pans): Lining baking pans with aluminum foil is a great way to avoid messy clean up whenever you bake bar cookies. Doing so also makes it easy to remove the entire batch of brownies or bars from the pan at once, making the cutting of perfectly uniform squares and bars a snap. When bars are cool or nearly cool, simply lift them out of the pan, peel back the foil and cut. Foil-lining is also a boon during holiday baking seasons, allowing for the production of multiple batches of bars and brownies in no time, with virtually no clean up.

Foil-lining is simple. Begin by turning the pan upside down. Tear off a piece of aluminum foil longer than the pan, and shape the foil over the pan. Carefully remove the foil and set aside. Flip the pan over and gently fit the shaped foil into the pan, allowing the foil to hang over the sides (the overhang ends will work as "handles" when the brownies or bars are removed).

Essential Utensils Checklist

✓ Dry measuring cups in graduated sizes ¼, ⅓, ½, and 1 cup

✓ Liquid measuring cup (preferably clear glass or plastic)

✓ Measuring spoons in graduated sizes ¼, ½, and 1 teaspoon as well as 1 tablespoon

- ✓ Wooden spoon(s)
- ✓ Mixing bowls (at least one each of small, medium, and large sizes)
- ✓ Rubber or silicone spatula (for scraping the sides of a mixing bowl)
- ✓ Metal spatula or pancake turner for removing cookies from sheets and bars from pans (use a plastic spatula if you are using a nonstick cookie sheet or baking pan)
- ✓ Wire cooling racks
- ✓ Oven mitts or holders
- ✓ Kitchen timer
- ✓ Cutting board
- ✓ Pastry brush (a clean 1-inch paintbrush from the hardware store works fine)
- ✓ Rolling pin
- ✓ Wire whisk
- ✓ Chef's knife
- ✓ Kitchen spoons (everyday place setting soup and teaspoons for drop cookies)
- ✓ Electric mixer (handheld or stand mixer)

Wish-List Utensils Checklist

- ✓ Small off-set metal spatula (ideal for frosting both cookies and bars)
- ✓ Metal pastry scraper (the perfect tool for cutting perfect squares and bars)
- ✓ Cookie scoops (look like small ice cream scoops—use for perfectly measured drop cookies)
- ✓ Food processor
- ✓ Cookie cutters
- ✓ Silicone cookie sheet liners (eliminates nonstick spray or greasing step)
- ✓ Zester

Baking Equipment Checklist

- ✓ 13 x 9-inch plain aluminum rectangular pan
- ✓ 15 x 10-inch jelly roll pan
- ✓ Plain aluminum cookie sheets (at least two)
- ✓ Madeleine pan (3 x 1¼-inch shell molds)

ONE

Drop Cookies

Blue-Ribbon Chocolate-Chip Cookies

Hats off to Ruth Wakefield. Back in the 1930s the clever home baker and proprietor of the Toll House Inn "invented" (whether by mistake or design—the jury is still out on this one) what we now know as the chocolate-chip cookie. American cookie baking has never been the same since, and thank goodness. This quick and easy cake mix version of Mrs. Wakefield's classic creation earns its blue-ribbon tag.

1	18.25-ounce package yellow cake mix
½	cup (1 stick) butter, softened
3	tablespoons packed dark brown sugar
2	large eggs
2	teaspoons vanilla extract
1½	cups semisweet chocolate chips
1	cup chopped pecans (or walnuts), optional

Preheat oven to 350°. Position oven rack in middle of oven. Spray cookie sheets with nonstick cooking spray.

In a large mixing bowl place half of the cake mix along with the softened butter, brown sugar, eggs, and vanilla extract. Blend with an electric mixer set on medium-high speed 1–2 minutes, until blended and smooth. Stir in the remaining cake mix, chocolate chips, and nuts, if desired, with a wooden spoon until all dry ingredients are moistened.

Drop by teaspoonfuls, 2 inches apart, onto prepared cookie sheets.

Bake 10–13 minutes or until golden at the edges and just barely set at center when lightly touched. Cool 1 minute on sheets. Transfer to wire racks with metal spatula and cool completely.

Variations:

Ginger Chocolate Chippers: Prepare as directed above but do not use nuts and add 1½ teaspoons ground ginger and ½ cup chopped crystallized ginger to the dough.

Tart Cherry Milk Chocolate Chippers: Prepare as directed above but replace semisweet chocolate chips with milk chocolate chips and add ⅔ cup dried tart cherries or dried cranberries instead of nuts.

Chocolate Mint Chocolate Chippers: Prepare as directed above but replace the vanilla extract with ¾ teaspoon peppermint extract. Sprinkle cookie tops with crushed red and white striped peppermint candies or candy canes just before baking (about 1 cup total).

Mocha Chocolate Chippers: Prepare as directed above but dissolve 1 tablespoon instant espresso or coffee powder in the vanilla extract before adding.

Toffee Chocolate Chippers: Prepare as directed above but add ¾ cup toffee baking bits to the dough instead of nuts.

Makes about 4½ dozen cookies.

Big Fat Oatmeal-Raisin Cookies

Oatmeal cookies are a nostalgic choice anytime. The brown sugar, vanilla extract, and butter heighten the rich, old-fashioned flavor of these easily assembled goodies. And if you're fond of a little innovation, try one or both of the variations, too, for a delicious punch of new flavor.

1	18.25-ounce package spice cake mix
⅓	cup packed dark brown sugar
1	cup (2 sticks) butter, softened
2	large eggs
2	teaspoons vanilla extract
1¼	cups raisins
2	cups quick-cooking oats

Preheat oven to 350°. Spray cookie sheets with nonstick cooking spray.

In a large mixing bowl place half of the cake mix along with the brown sugar, softened butter, eggs, vanilla extract, and raisins. Blend with an electric mixer set on medium-high speed 1–2 minutes, until blended and smooth. Stir in the remaining cake mix and oats with a wooden spoon until all dry ingredients are well blended (dough will be very stiff).

Drop dough by level ¼-cupfuls, 2 inches apart, onto prepared cookie sheets; flatten slightly with the bottom of a glass.

Bake 13–17 minutes or until set at edges and just barely set at center when lightly touched. Cool 1 minute on sheets. Transfer to wire racks with metal spatula and cool completely.

Variations:
Cranberry-Orange Oatmeal Cookies: Prepare as directed above but replace raisins with dried cranberries and add 1 tablespoon grated orange zest.

Tropical Oatmeal Cookies: Prepare as directed above but replace raisins with dried tropical fruit bits and add 1 teaspoon ground ginger and 1 tablespoon grated lime zest.

Makes 2 dozen big cookies.

Premium White Chocolate Macadamia Cookies

Premium indeed. White chocolate macadamia cookies appeared on the culinary scene in the 1980s and have been favorites ever since. Make a batch to remind yourself of what all of the hype is about. And if macadamia nuts are unavailable, pretty much any other nut will work in their place.

1   18.25-ounce package yellow cake mix
1   cup all purpose flour
¾   cup (1½ sticks) butter, melted
¼   cup packed light brown sugar
2   large eggs
2   teaspoons vanilla extract
¾   cup quick-cooking oats
1   cup coarsely chopped macadamia nuts
1⅓ cups white chocolate chips

Preheat oven to 350°. Position oven rack in middle of oven. Set aside ungreased cookie sheets.

In a large mixing bowl place the cake mix, flour, melted butter, brown sugar, eggs, and vanilla extract. Blend with an electric mixer set on medium-high speed 1–2 minutes, until blended and smooth. Stir in the oats, nuts, and white chocolate chips with a wooden spoon until all dry ingredients are moistened.

Drop dough by teaspoonfuls, 2 inches apart, onto cookie sheets.

Bake 10–13 minutes, until golden at edges and just barely set at center when lightly touched. Cool 1 minute on sheets. Transfer to wire racks with metal spatula and cool completely.

Variations:

Coffee & White Chocolate Macadamia Cookies: Prepare as directed above but dissolve 2 and ½ teaspoons instant espresso or coffee powder in the vanilla extract before adding to the batter.

Lemony White Chocolate Macadamia Cookies: Prepare as directed above but use 2 tablespoons grated lemon zest in place of the vanilla extract.

Makes about 4½ dozen cookies.

Premium White Chocolate Macadamia Cookies

Bittersweet Chocolate Blackout Cookies

The list of what's great about these very chocolate, crisp-chewy cookies is long. In addition to an over-the-top chocolate intensity, they're quite practical: you can make several dozen premium cookies with a few flicks of a spoon and have a delicious chocolate bounty ready and waiting.

2	tablespoons instant espresso or coffee powder
⅓	cup water
1	18.25-ounce package devil's food cake mix
¼	cup (½ stick) butter, melted
1	large egg
1	8-ounce package bittersweet baking chocolate, coarsely chopped into chunks

Preheat oven to 350°. Position oven rack in middle of oven. Spray cookie sheets with nonstick cooking spray.

In a large mixing bowl combine the espresso powder and water, stirring to dissolve. To the same bowl add half of the cake mix along with the melted butter and egg. Blend with an electric mixer set on medium-high speed 1–2 minutes, until blended and smooth. Stir in the remaining cake mix and chopped chocolate with a wooden spoon until all dry ingredients are moistened.

Drop dough by teaspoonfuls, 2 inches apart, on prepared cookie sheets.

Bake 9–12 minutes or until set at edges and just barely set at center when lightly touched. Cool 1 minute on sheets. Transfer to wire racks with metal spatula and cool completely.

Variation:

Black & White Blackout Cookies: Prepare as directed above but substitute 1 6-ounce package chopped white chocolate baking bars for bittersweet chocolate.

Makes about 4 dozen cookies.

Apple-Cranberry Harvest Cookies

*Cranberries, apples, and nuts, covered in a quick and spicy dough, make
for a festive, fuss-free cookie. If other nuts, such as almonds or pecans, are
what you have on hand, use them interchangeably with the walnuts, or leave
them out altogether if you prefer.*

1	18.25-ounce package spice cake mix
1	teaspoon ground cinnamon
⅓	cup vegetable oil
2	large eggs
1	cup peeled and finely chopped tart apple (e.g., Granny Smith)
⅔	cup dried cranberries
1	cup chopped walnuts

Preheat oven to 350°. Position oven rack in middle of oven. Spray cookie sheets with
nonstick cooking spray.

In a large mixing bowl place half of the cake mix along with the cinnamon, oil, and
eggs. Blend with an electric mixer set on medium-high speed 1–2 minutes, until
blended and smooth. Stir in the remaining cake mix, apple and cranberries with a
wooden spoon until all dry ingredients are moistened.

Drop dough by teaspoonfuls, 2 inches apart, on prepared cookie sheets. Sprinkle
tops with a few chopped walnuts; gently press into the dough.

Bake 9–12 minutes or until set at edges and just barely set at center when lightly
touched. Cool 1 minute on sheets. Transfer to wire racks with metal spatula and cool
completely.

Makes about 4½ dozen cookies.

Gingerbread Softies

*As the weather grows colder and the holidays head in, there's
no better time to bake a batch of the kind of cookies that
fill every room in the house with the familiar scents
of good things to come. These cookies, redolent with
sweet vanilla, spicy ginger, and cinnamon, fit the bill.*

1	18.25-ounce package spice cake mix
1	8-ounce package cream cheese, softened
¼	cup (½ stick) butter, melted
1	large egg
¼	cup packed dark brown sugar
2	teaspoons ground ginger
¾	teaspoon ground cinnamon
2	teaspoons vanilla extract
1	recipe Orange or Lemon Icing (page 213), optional

Preheat oven to 350°. Position oven rack in middle of oven. Spray cookie sheets with
nonstick cooking spray.

In a large mixing bowl place half of the cake mix along with the softened cream
cheese, melted butter, egg, brown sugar, ginger, cinnamon, and vanilla extract. Blend
with an electric mixer set on medium-high speed 1–2 minutes, until blended and
smooth. Stir in the remaining cake mix with a wooden spoon until all dry ingredients
are moistened.

Drop by teaspoonfuls, 2 inches apart, onto prepared cookie sheets.

Bake 10–13 minutes or until just barely set at center when lightly touched. Cool
1 minute on sheets. Transfer to wire racks with metal spatula and cool completely.

If desired, prepare Orange or Lemon Icing. Drizzle icing over cooled cookies.

Makes about 4½ dozen cookies.

Toasted Almond Cookies

Five ingredients—that's all it takes to produce these elegant, and very almond, cookies. They are a fine choice for teatime.

1   18.25-ounce package vanilla cake mix
⅓   cup vegetable oil
2   large eggs
1   teaspoon almond extract
1⅓ cups sliced almonds

Preheat oven to 350°. Position oven rack in middle of oven. Spray cookie sheets with nonstick cooking spray.

In a large mixing bowl place half of the cake mix along with the oil, eggs, and almond extract. Blend with an electric mixer set on medium-high speed 1–2 minutes, until blended and smooth. Stir in the remaining cake mix with a wooden spoon until all dry ingredients are moistened.

Drop dough by teaspoonfuls, 2 inches apart, onto prepared cookie sheets. Sprinkle cookie tops with sliced almonds; gently press almonds into dough.

Bake 9–12 minutes or until set at edges and just barely set at center when lightly touched. Cool 1 minute on sheets. Transfer to wire racks with metal spatula and cool completely.

Makes about 4 dozen cookies.

Praline Cookies

This is one great cookie. The dough will spread out relatively thin as it bakes because the butter recipe cake mix has a higher fat content than other cake mixes. It is very important to let the cookies rest on the sheets before transferring them to cooling racks (they will be too soft when they first come out of the oven). The result is a thin, crispy cookie that really does taste like a praline. For a perfectly round cookie, try using a cookie scoop—it looks like a mini ice cream scooper. I bet once you taste these you'll agree that a praline in cookie form tastes just as sweet.

1	18.25-ounce package butter recipe cake mix
½	cup (1 stick) butter, softened
¼	cup packed dark brown sugar
2	large eggs
1	teaspoon vanilla extract
1¼	cups toffee baking bits
2	cups chopped pecans

Preheat oven to 350°. Position oven rack in middle of oven. Spray cookie sheets with nonstick cooking spray.

In a large mixing bowl place half of the cake mix along with the softened butter, brown sugar, eggs, and vanilla extract. Blend with an electric mixer set on medium-high speed 1–2 minutes, until blended and smooth. Stir in the remaining cake mix and toffee bits with a wooden spoon until all dry ingredients are moistened.

Drop by teaspoonfuls, 2 inches apart, onto prepared cookie sheets. Generously sprinkle cookie tops with chopped pecans; gently press into cookies.

Bake 10–12 minutes or until golden brown at edges. Cool 2 minutes on sheets. Transfer to wire racks with metal spatula and cool completely.

Makes about 4½ dozen cookies.

Piña Colada Cookies

*All of the flavors of the cool, creamy tropical drink come together
in this easy, breezy cookie.*

1   8-ounce package cream cheese, softened
¼   cup (½ stick) butter, softened
1   large egg yolk
½   cup pineapple juice
2   teaspoons rum-flavored extract
1   18.25-ounce package yellow cake mix
1   cup sweetened flaked coconut

In a large mixing bowl place the softened cream cheese and softened butter. Blend
with an electric mixer set on medium-high speed 1–2 minutes, until blended and
smooth. Add the egg yolk, pineapple juice, rum extract, and half of the cake mix;
blend with an electric mixer set on medium-high speed 1–2 minutes, until blended and
smooth. Stir in the remaining cake mix and coconut with a wooden spoon until all dry
ingredients are moistened. Chill dough, covered, 30 minutes.

Preheat oven to 375°. Position oven rack in middle of oven. Spray cookie sheets
with nonstick cooking spray.

Drop dough by teaspoonfuls, 2 inches apart, onto prepared cookie sheets.

Bake 9–11 minutes or until set at edges and just barely set at center when lightly
touched. Cool 1 minute on sheets. Transfer to wire racks with metal spatula and cool
completely.

Makes about 4 dozen cookies.

Neapolitan Cookies

*These tricolor cookies are as delightful and delicious as the
brick ice cream by the same name.*

1	18.25-ounce package cherry chip cake mix
¼	cup vegetable oil
2	tablespoons water
2	large eggs
½	teaspoon almond extract
¾	cup finely chopped maraschino cherries (patted dry between paper towels)
1	cup miniature semisweet chocolate chips

Preheat oven to 350°. Position oven rack in middle of oven. Spray cookie sheets with nonstick cooking spray.

In a large mixing bowl place half of the cake mix along with the oil, water, eggs, and almond extract. Blend with an electric mixer set on medium-high speed 1–2 minutes, until blended and smooth. Stir in the remaining cake mix, cherries, and chocolate chips with a wooden spoon until all dry ingredients are moistened.

Drop by teaspoonfuls, 2 inches apart, onto prepared cookie sheets.

Bake 10–12 minutes or until golden brown at edges. Cool 1 minute on sheets. Transfer to wire racks with metal spatula and cool completely.

Makes about 4½ dozen cookies.

Peanut Butter Cookies

There's a time for discovering new flavors and a time for savoring old favorites. When you're in the mood for the latter, whip up a batch of these peanut butter cookies.

1   **cup creamy peanut butter (not old-fashioned or natural style)**
2   **large eggs**
⅓   **cup milk**
1   **18.25-ounce package yellow cake mix**
⅓   **cup granulated sugar**

Preheat oven to 375°. Position oven rack in middle of oven. Spray cookie sheets with nonstick cooking spray.

In a large mixing bowl mix the peanut butter, eggs, milk, and half of the cake mix with a wooden spoon until well blended. Mix in remaining cake mix with a spoon until blended and all dry ingredients are moistened.

Place sugar in a shallow dish. Drop dough by tablespoonfuls onto prepared cookie sheets. Gently press a crisscross pattern on top of cookies with fork dipped in the sugar.

Bake 10–12 minutes or until set at edges and just barely set at center when lightly touched. Cool 3–4 minutes on sheets to firm the cookies. Transfer to wire racks with metal spatula and cool completely.

Makes about 4 dozen cookies.

Walnut-Date Cookies

Dates are one of the first confections, going back more than 5000 years in culinary history. Although native to the Middle East, they are also plentiful in my home state of California. For anyone who loves brown sugar (me!), dates are a favorite cookie ingredient. Here they add a toothsome chewiness, a delicious foil to the nutty crunch of walnuts.

1   18.25-ounce package vanilla cake mix
¾   cup (1½ sticks) butter, melted
⅓   cup all-purpose flour
2   large eggs
1   teaspoon ground cinnamon
1   cup quick-cooking oats
1   cup chopped dates
1   cup chopped walnuts

Preheat oven to 375°. Position oven rack in middle of oven. Spray cookie sheets with nonstick cooking spray.

In a large mixing bowl place half of the cake mix along with the melted butter, flour, eggs, and cinnamon. Blend with an electric mixer set on medium-high speed 1–2 minutes, until blended and smooth. Stir in the remaining cake mix, oats, and dates with a wooden spoon until all dry ingredients are moistened.

Drop dough by teaspoonfuls, 2 inches apart, onto prepared cookie sheets. Sprinkle cookie tops with a few chopped walnuts.

Bake 9–11 minutes or until set at edges and just barely set at center when lightly touched. Cool 1 minute on sheets. Transfer to wire racks with metal spatula and cool completely.

Makes about 5½ dozen cookies.

Peanut Butter Chocolate Chunkers

A scrumptious pairing of dark chocolate and peanut butter, these chunky cookies call for tall glasses of cold milk and lots of good cheer.

1   18.25-ounce package chocolate cake mix
½   cup chunky-style peanut butter (not old-fashioned or natural style)
½   cup (1 stick) butter, softened
3   large eggs
1   cup semisweet chocolate chips or chunks

Preheat oven to 350°. Position oven rack in middle of oven. Spray cookie sheets with nonstick cooking spray.

In a large mixing bowl place half of the cake mix along with the peanut butter, softened butter, and eggs. Blend with an electric mixer set on medium-high speed 1–2 minutes, until blended and smooth. Stir in the remaining cake mix and chocolate chips with a wooden spoon until all dry ingredients are moistened.

Drop dough by teaspoonfuls, 2 inches apart, onto prepared cookie sheets.

Bake 10–13 minutes or until set at edges and just barely set at center when lightly touched. Cool 1 minute on sheets. Transfer to wire racks with metal spatula and cool completely.

Makes about 4 dozen cookies.

"I Love Lime" White Chocolate Cookies

If ever a match was made in culinary heaven, it is lime and white chocolate. These particular cookies, as their eponym suggests, are loaded with lime—both the juice in the icing and the zest in the cookies—and balanced by the smooth sweetness of the white chocolate chips that stud each treat.

1	18.25-ounce package vanilla cake mix
½	cup (1 stick) butter, softened
2	large eggs
1	tablespoon grated lime zest
1¼	cups white chocolate chips
1	recipe Lime Icing (see page 213)

Preheat oven to 350°. Position oven rack in upper third of oven. Spray cookie sheets with nonstick cooking spray.

In a large mixing bowl place half of the cake mix, softened butter, eggs, and lime zest. Blend with an electric mixer set on medium-high speed 1–2 minutes, until blended and smooth. Stir in the remaining cake mix and white chocolate chips with a wooden spoon until all dry ingredients are moistened.

Drop dough by teaspoonfuls, 2 inches apart, onto prepared cookie sheets.

Bake 10–13 minutes or until set at edges and just barely set at center when lightly touched. Cool 1 minute on sheets. Transfer to wire racks with metal spatula and cool completely. Prepare Lime Icing. Drizzle icing over cooled cookies.

Variation:

"I Love Lemon" White Chocolate Cookies: Prepare as directed above but substitute lemon zest for the lime zest and Lemon Icing (see page 213) for the Lime Icing.

Makes about 4 dozen cookies.

Rum Raisin Cookies

Enhanced with the flavors of rum and nutmeg, these easy raisin cookies are fit for both company and comfort on a cold, chilly night.

1	18.25-ounce package yellow cake mix
½	teaspoon ground nutmeg
⅓	cup vegetable oil
2	large eggs
1½	teaspoons rum extract
1½	cups raisins
1	recipe Rum Icing (see page 217)

Preheat oven to 350°. Position oven rack in middle of oven. Spray cookie sheets with nonstick cooking spray.

In a large mixing bowl place half of the cake mix along with the nutmeg, oil, eggs, and rum extract. Blend with an electric mixer set on medium-high speed 1–2 minutes, until blended and smooth. Stir in the remaining cake mix and raisins with a wooden spoon until all dry ingredients are moistened.

Drop dough by teaspoonfuls, 2 inches apart, on prepared cookie sheets.

Bake 9–12 minutes or until set at edges and just barely set at center when lightly touched. Cool 1 minute on sheets. Transfer to wire racks with metal spatula and cool completely.

Prepare Rum Icing. Drizzle icing over cooled cookies.

Variation:

Brandied Apricot Cookies: Prepare as directed above but substitute snipped dried apricots for the raisins, brandy extract for the rum extract, and Brandy Icing (see page 217) for the Rum Icing.

Makes about 4½ dozen cookies.

Peaches & Cream Cookies

You'll taste the best of summer when you bite into these peachy-keen cookies. Although irresistible frosted, they are excellent straight-up, too.

1   18.25-ounce package vanilla cake mix
½   cup vegetable oil
½   cup peach preserves
1   tablespoon grated lemon zest
1   large egg
1   recipe Cream Cheese Frosting (see page 212)

Preheat oven to 350°. Position oven rack in upper third of oven. Spray cookie sheets with nonstick cooking spray.

In a large mixing bowl place half of the cake mix along with the oil, preserves, lemon zest, and egg. Blend with an electric mixer set on medium-high speed 1–2 minutes, until blended and smooth. Stir in the remaining cake mix with a wooden spoon until all dry ingredients are moistened.

Drop dough by teaspoonfuls, 2 inches apart, onto prepared cookie sheets.

Bake 11–13 minutes or until set at edges and just golden brown. Cool 1 minute on sheets. Transfer to wire racks with metal spatula and cool completely. Prepare Cream Cheese Frosting; frost cookies.

Variations:

Frosted Apricot Cookies: Prepare as directed above but use apricot preserves in place of the peach preserves and add ¼ teaspoon ground nutmeg to the dough along with the other ingredients.

Marmalade Spice Cookies: Prepare as directed above but eliminate the lemon zest, use a spice cake mix in place of the vanilla cake mix, use orange marmalade in place of the peach preserves, and add ¾ teaspoon ground cinnamon to the dough along with the other ingredients.

Makes about 4 dozen cookies.

Fresh Pear Cookies
with Browned Butter Icing

Here a great cookie, loaded with fresh pears and a sprinkle of nutmeg, gets even better with the addition of a quick slick of Browned Butter Icing. Be sure to use real butter—margarine does not get brown and nutty the way real butter will. It's not necessary to peel the pears before chopping and adding to the dough.

1	18.25-ounce package vanilla cake mix
½	cup (1 stick) butter, softened
¼	cup packed light brown sugar
2	large eggs
¾	teaspoon ground nutmeg
1½	cups coarsely chopped fresh pears (about 2 medium pears)
1	cup finely chopped pecans
1	recipe Browned Butter Icing (see page 214)

Preheat oven to 350°. Position oven rack in middle of oven. Spray cookie sheets with nonstick cooking spray.

In a large mixing bowl place half of the cake mix along with the softened butter, brown sugar, eggs, and nutmeg. Blend with an electric mixer set on medium-high speed 1–2 minutes, until blended and smooth. Stir in the remaining cake mix and pears with a wooden spoon until all dry ingredients are moistened.

Drop by teaspoonfuls, 2 inches apart, onto prepared cookie sheets. Sprinkle cookie tops with pecans.

Bake 10–13 minutes or until cracked in appearance and just barely set at center when lightly touched. Cool 1 minute on sheets. Transfer to wire racks with metal spatula and cool completely. Prepare Browned Butter Icing; drizzle over cooled cookies.

Variations:

Fresh Cranberry Cookies: Prepare as directed above but replace the fresh pears with an equal amount of coarsely chopped fresh cranberries and replace the nutmeg with an equal amount of ground ginger.

Fresh Apple Cookies: Prepare as directed above but replace the fresh pears with an equal amount of coarsely chopped peeled tart apples and replace the nutmeg with an equal amount of ground cinnamon.

Makes about 4 dozen cookies.

Fresh Pear Cookies with Browned Butter Icing

Cranberry Cornmeal Cookies

If ever there was a Thanksgiving cookie, this is it. Cornmeal adds both crunch and color, a fine counterpoint to tart, red, chewy bits of cranberry.

1	18.25-ounce package yellow cake mix
⅔	cup plain yellow cornmeal
⅓	cup vegetable oil
2	large eggs
1	tablespoon grated lemon or orange zest
1¼	cups sweetened dried cranberries, chopped

Preheat oven to 350°. Position oven rack in middle of oven. Spray cookie sheets with nonstick cooking spray.

In a large mixing bowl place half of the cake mix along with the the cornmeal, oil, eggs, and zest. Blend with an electric mixer set on medium-high speed 1–2 minutes, until blended and smooth. Stir in the remaining cake mix and dried cranberries with a wooden spoon until all dry ingredients are moistened.

Drop dough by teaspoonfuls, 2 inches apart, onto prepared cookie sheets.

Bake 9–12 minutes or until set at edges and just barely set at center when lightly touched. Cool 1 minute on sheets. Transfer to wire racks with metal spatula and cool completely.

Makes about 4 dozen cookies.

Granola Chocolate Chunkers

Excellent travelers, these sturdy cookies are a good choice for care packages, lunch boxes, and also backpacks when heading out on a hike or picnic.

1   **18.25-ounce package yellow cake mix**
¼   **cup packed brown sugar**
½   **cup vegetable oil**
2   **large eggs**
2   **teaspoons vanilla extract**
1½ **cups granola**
¾   **cup dried fruit of choice (e.g., raisins, dried cranberries, chopped dried apricots)**
1   **cup semisweet chocolate chunks**

Preheat oven to 350°. Position oven rack in middle of oven. Spray cookie sheets with nonstick cooking spray.

In a large mixing bowl place half of the cake mix along with the brown sugar, oil, eggs, and vanilla extract. Blend with an electric mixer set on medium-high speed 1–2 minutes, until blended and smooth. Stir in the remaining cake mix, granola, dried fruit, and chocolate chunks with a wooden spoon until all dry ingredients are moistened.

Drop dough by teaspoonfuls, 2 inches apart, onto prepared cookie sheets.

Bake 9–12 minutes or until set at edges and just barely set at center when lightly touched. Cool 1 minute on sheets. Transfer to wire racks with metal spatula and cool completely.

Makes about 5½ dozen cookies.

Iced Maple-Pecan Cookies

Looking for a new Christmas cookie? Give these double-maple treats a try—they're sure to become a fast family favorite, especially if you pair them with mugs of hot cocoa.

1   18.25-ounce package butter pecan cake mix
⅓   cup butter, softened
2   large eggs
2   teaspoons maple extract
1   cup chopped pecans
1   recipe Maple Icing (see page 216)

Preheat oven to 350°. Position oven rack in middle of oven. Spray cookie sheets with nonstick cooking spray.

In a large mixing bowl place half of the cake mix along with the softened butter, eggs, and maple extract. Blend with an electric mixer set on medium-high speed 1–2 minutes, until blended and smooth. Stir in the remaining cake mix and pecans with a wooden spoon until all dry ingredients are moistened.

Drop dough by teaspoonfuls, 2 inches apart, onto prepared cookie sheets.

Bake 9–12 minutes or until set at edges and just barely set at center when lightly touched. Cool 1 minute on sheets. Transfer to wire racks with metal spatula and cool completely.

Prepare Maple Icing. Drizzle icing over cookies.

Makes about 4½ dozen cookies.

Caramel-loaded Chocolate-Chocolate-Chip Cookies

Chocolate-coated caramel candies sweeten the deal in these incredible double chocolate chippers. They are over-the-top good when eaten slightly warm, while the caramel and chocolate are still a bit gooey.

1	cup quartered chocolate-covered caramel candies (e.g., Rolos®)
2	tablespoons all-purpose flour
1	18.25-ounce package yellow or chocolate cake mix
⅓	cup vegetable oil
2	large eggs
1	cup semisweet or milk chocolate chips

Preheat oven to 350°. Position oven rack in middle of oven. Spray cookie sheets with nonstick cooking spray.

In a small bowl toss the chopped candies with flour (to prevent sticking).

In a large mixing bowl place half of the cake mix along with the oil and eggs. Blend with an electric mixer set on medium-high speed 1–2 minutes, until blended and smooth. Stir in the remaining cake mix, flour-coated candies, and chocolate chips with a wooden spoon until all dry ingredients are moistened.

Drop dough by teaspoonfuls, 2 inches apart, onto prepared cookie sheets.

Bake 9–12 minutes or until set at edges and just barely set at center when lightly touched. Cool 1 minute on sheets. Transfer to wire racks with metal spatula and cool completely.

Makes about 4½ dozen cookies.

Pine Nut Cookies

Pine nuts, also known as pignola, pignoli, Indian nuts, and pinon, come from the pine cones of several varieties of pine trees. Sweet and delicate in flavor, the ivory-colored, torpedo-shaped nuts are used in a wide array of savory and sweet dishes in many cuisines. They are particularly delicious in baked goods, like these subtly spiced, Italian-inspired cookies. Anise is a traditional flavoring in Italian baked goods, but 1/2 teaspoon ground nutmeg, mace, or coriander in may be substituted.

1	18.25-ounce package vanilla cake mix
½	cup (1 stick) butter, softened
2	large eggs
1	teaspoon vanilla extract
1	teaspoon anise seed, coarsely crushed in a mortar and pestle
1	cup pine nuts

Preheat oven to 350°. Position oven rack in upper third of oven. Spray cookie sheets with nonstick cooking spray.

In a large mixing bowl place half of the cake mix along with the softened butter, eggs, vanilla extract, and anise seed. Blend with an electric mixer set on medium-high speed 1–2 minutes, until blended and smooth. Stir in the remaining cake mix with a wooden spoon until all dry ingredients are moistened.

Drop dough by teaspoonfuls, 2 inches apart, onto prepared cookie sheets. Sprinkle cookie tops with a few pine nuts; gently press nuts into dough.

Bake 9–12 minutes or until set at edges and just barely set at center when lightly touched. Cool 1 minute on sheets. Transfer to wire racks with metal spatula and cool completely.

Makes about 4½ dozen cookies.

Pineapple Softies

This friendly cookie is an ideal choice for giving to new friends and neighbors because it is lush with pineapple, the historic symbol of welcome.

1   18.25-ounce package spice cake mix
1   8-ounce can crushed pineapple, drained, juice reserved
¼   cup vegetable oil
1   large egg
1   cup sweetened flaked coconut, optional

Preheat oven to 350°. Position oven rack in middle of oven. Spray cookie sheets with nonstick cooking spray.

In a large mixing bowl place half of the cake mix along with the pineapple, 2 tablespoons of the reserved juice, oil, and egg. Blend with an electric mixer set on medium-high speed 1–2 minutes, until blended and smooth. Stir in the remaining cake mix with a wooden spoon until all dry ingredients are moistened.

Drop dough by teaspoonfuls, 2 inches apart, onto prepared cookie sheets. If desired, sprinkle cookie tops with coconut; gently press into dough.

Bake 10–13 minutes or until set at edges and just barely set at center when lightly touched. Cool 1 minute on sheets. Transfer to wire racks with metal spatula and cool completely.

Makes about 4 dozen cookies.

Chai Spice Cookies

*These quick cookies capture the unique flavor of chai,
an aromatic spiced tea drink long favored in the East Indies.
Warm and wonderful, they will fill the house with their distinctive
fragrance as they bake.*

1	18.25-ounce package spice cake mix
⅓	cup butter, melted
2	large eggs
2	teaspoons pumpkin pie spice
½	teaspoon ground cardamom
1	cup slivered almonds
1	recipe Vanilla Icing (see page 216), optional

Preheat oven to 350°. Position oven rack in middle of oven. Spray cookie sheets with nonstick cooking spray.

In a large mixing bowl place half of the cake mix along with the melted butter, eggs, pumpkin pie spice, and cardamom. Blend with an electric mixer set on medium-high speed 1–2 minutes, until blended and smooth. Stir in the remaining cake mix with a wooden spoon until all dry ingredients are moistened.

Drop dough by teaspoonfuls, 2 inches apart, onto prepared cookie sheets. Sprinkle cookie tops with a few slivered almonds.

Bake 9–12 minutes or until set at edges and just barely set at center when lightly touched. Cool 1 minute on sheets. Transfer to wire racks with metal spatula and cool completely. If desired, prepare Vanilla Icing; drizzle over cooled cookies.

Makes about 4½ dozen cookies.

Ricotta Cookies

Somewhat similar to cottage cheese, ricotta is a slightly grainy, very soft, and smooth Italian cheese used in a variety of sweet and savory dishes like cheesecake and lasagna. Here it creates a rich, cake-like cookie with a crisp shell and soft, snowy interior. For a citrus variation, substitute 2 teaspoons of freshly grated lemon, lime, or orange zest for the vanilla.

1	**18.25-ounce package vanilla cake mix**
¼	**cup (½ stick) butter, melted**
¾	**cup ricotta cheese**
1	**large egg**
2	**teaspoons vanilla extract**
1	**recipe Vanilla Icing (see page 216)**

Preheat oven to 350°. Position oven rack in middle of oven.

In a large mixing bowl place half of the cake mix along with the melted butter, ricotta cheese, egg, and vanilla extract. Blend with an electric mixer set on medium-high speed 1–2 minutes, until blended and smooth. Stir in the remaining cake mix with a wooden spoon until all dry ingredients are moistened (dough will be somewhat stiff).

Drop dough by teaspoonfuls, 2 inches apart, onto ungreased cookie sheets.

Bake 9–12 minutes or until golden at edges and just barely set at center when lightly touched (do not overbake; cookies will become more firm as they cool). Transfer to wire rack and cool completely.

Prepare Vanilla Icing. Drizzle cooled cookies with icing.

Makes 4 dozen cookies.

Eggnog Cookies

Here that homogenous blend of eggs, cream, spices, spirits, and plenty of holiday cheer finds form in a delectable, streamlined cookie. For a dazzling finish, drizzle with or dip in melted white or dark chocolate (see page 206).

1	18.25-ounce package yellow cake mix
⅓	cup butter, melted
2	large eggs
2	teaspoons brandy or rum-flavored extract
2	teaspoons ground nutmeg, divided
½	teaspoon ground cinnamon
⅓	cup sugar

Preheat oven to 350°. Position oven rack in middle of oven. Spray cookie sheets with nonstick cooking spray.

In a large mixing bowl place half of the cake mix along with the melted butter, eggs, extract, 1 teaspoon nutmeg, and cinnamon. Blend with an electric mixer set on medium-high speed 1–2 minutes, until blended and smooth. Stir in the remaining cake mix with a wooden spoon until all dry ingredients are moistened.

In a small dish combine the sugar and remaining teaspoon nutmeg. Drop dough by teaspoonfuls, 2 inches apart, onto prepared cookie sheets; sprinkle cookie tops with the nutmeg sugar.

Bake 9–12 minutes or until set at edges and just barely set at center when lightly touched. Cool 1 minute on sheets. Transfer to wire racks with metal spatula and cool completely.

Makes about 4½ dozen cookies.

Brandied Fruitcake Jumbles

There's no middle ground when it comes to fruitcake—one person's beloved portent of the Christmas season is another's bitter pill. But there's no better cookie than this brandy-accented one to convince even the most stalwart of skeptics.

1	**18.25-ounce package yellow cake mix**
¼	**cup brandy or dark rum**
¼	**cup (½ stick) butter, melted**
1	**large egg**
½	**cup quick-cooking oats**
⅔	**cup raisins**
1	**cup candied cherries, chopped**
1	**cup chopped walnuts (or pecans)**

Preheat oven to 350°. Position oven rack in middle of oven. Spray cookie sheets with nonstick cooking spray.

In a large mixing bowl place half of the cake mix along with the brandy, melted butter, egg, and oats. Blend with an electric mixer set on medium-high speed 1–2 minutes, until blended and smooth. Stir in the remaining cake mix, raisins, and candied cherries with a wooden spoon until all dry ingredients are moistened.

Drop dough by teaspoonfuls, 2 inches apart, onto prepared cookie sheets. Sprinkle cookie tops with nuts; gently press nuts into dough.

Bake 10–13 minutes or until just barely set at center when lightly touched. Cool 1 minute on sheets. Transfer to wire racks with metal spatula and cool completely.

Makes about 4 dozen cookies.

Orange Dreamsicle Cookies

Remember those orange and vanilla cream pops from summer vacations past? Vanilla ice cream inside, orange sherbet outside, they always topped my list of ice pop favorites. Recapture that summertime flavor with these orange and vanilla cookies. But don't limit them to the summer months—they are delicious year-round.

1	18.25-ounce package yellow cake mix
½	cup (1 stick) butter, melted
1	large egg
1	tablespoon grated orange zest
1½	cups white chocolate chips
1	recipe Orange Icing (see page 213)

Preheat oven to 350°. Position oven rack in middle of oven.

In a large mixing bowl place half of the cake mix along with the melted butter, egg, and orange zest. Blend with an electric mixer set on medium-high speed 1–2 minutes, until blended and smooth. Stir in the remaining cake mix and white chocolate chips with a wooden spoon until all dry ingredients are moistened.

Drop dough by teaspoonfuls, 2 inches apart, onto ungreased cookie sheets.

Bake 10–13 minutes or until just barely set at center when lightly touched. Cool 1 minute on sheets. Transfer to wire racks with metal spatula and cool completely. Prepare Orange Icing. Drizzle icing over cooled cookies.

Makes about 4 dozen cookies.

Butterscotch Pecan Cookies

Butter pecan to the max! These cookies have magical properties—they disappear almost as quickly as they are made.

1   18.25-ounce package butter pecan cake mix
⅓   cup butter, melted
2   large eggs
1½   cups butterscotch baking chips
1⅓   cups chopped pecans

Preheat oven to 350°. Position oven rack in middle of oven. Spray cookie sheets with nonstick cooking spray.

In a large mixing bowl place half of the cake mix along with the melted butter and eggs. Blend with an electric mixer set on medium-high speed 1–2 minutes, until blended and smooth. Stir in the remaining cake mix and butterscotch baking chips with a wooden spoon until all dry ingredients are moistened.

Drop dough by teaspoonfuls, 2 inches apart, onto prepared cookie sheets. Sprinkle chopped pecans onto cookie tops; gently press nuts into dough.

Bake 9–12 minutes until set at edges and just barely set at center when lightly touched. Cool 1 minute on sheets. Transfer to wire racks with metal spatula and cool completely.

Makes about 4½ dozen cookies.

Carrot Cake Jumbles
with Cream Cheese Frosting

Looking for a friendly good time? Few things could be more conducive to such than, perhaps, the pure congeniality that comes from baking a batch of these carrot cookies, plump with fruit and spices and finished with a swirl of Cream Cheese Frosting.

1   18.25-ounce package carrot cake mix
⅓   cup vegetable oil
2   large eggs
1   teaspoon pumpkin pie spice
1½   cups grated peeled carrot (about 2 medium)
1   cup raisins (or dried cranberries)
½   cup canned crushed pineapple, well drained
1¼   cups finely chopped walnuts (or pecans), optional
1   recipe Cream Cheese Frosting (see page 212)

Preheat oven to 350°. Position oven rack in middle of oven. Spray cookie sheets with nonstick cooking spray.

In a large mixing bowl place half of the cake mix along with the oil, eggs, and pumpkin pie spice. Blend with an electric mixer set on medium-high speed 1–2 minutes, until blended and smooth. Stir in the remaining cake mix, grated carrot, raisins, and drained pineapple with a wooden spoon until all dry ingredients are moistened (dough will be stiff).

Drop dough by teaspoonfuls, 2 inches apart, onto prepared cookie sheets. If desired, sprinkle cookie tops with nuts; gently press nuts into dough.

Bake 11–14 minutes or until set at edges and just barely set at center when lightly touched. Cool 1 minute on sheets. Transfer to wire racks with metal spatula and cool completely.

Prepare Cream Cheese Frosting. Spread frosting over cooled cookies.

Makes about 4½ dozen cookies.

Lemon Poppyseed Cookies

Here's proof positive that joy can be shared in small, sweet ways. Impressive to serve, these lemon-y treats are equally easy to prepare.

1   18.25-ounce package lemon cake mix
⅓   cup vegetable oil
2   large eggs
1½   tablespoons grated lemon zest
3   tablespoons poppyseeds
1   recipe Lemon Icing (page 213), optional

Preheat oven to 350°. Position oven rack in middle of oven. Spray cookie sheets with nonstick cooking spray.

In a large mixing bowl place half of the cake mix along with the oil, eggs, lemon zest, and poppyseeds. Blend with an electric mixer set on medium-high speed 1–2 minutes, until blended and smooth. Stir in the remaining cake mix with a wooden spoon until all dry ingredients are moistened.

Drop dough by teaspoonfuls, 2 inches apart, onto prepared cookie sheets.

Bake 9–12 minutes or until set at edges and just barely set at center when lightly touched. Cool 1 minute on sheets. Transfer to wire racks with metal spatula and cool completely.

If desired, prepare Lemon Icing; drizzle icing over cooled cookies.

Makes about 4 dozen cookies.

Mandarin Orange Cookies

Looking for a very special cookie? Sweet-tart mandarin oranges and a bit of orange zest dress up a basic cake mix dough, transforming it from ordinary to extraordinary with minimal effort and expense.

1   18.25-ounce package yellow cake mix
⅓   cup vegetable oil
1   large egg
1   tablespoon grated orange zest
1   10-ounce can mandarin oranges, well drained, coarsely chopped
1   recipe Orange Icing (see page 213)

Preheat oven to 350°. Position oven rack in middle of oven. Spray cookie sheets with nonstick cooking spray.

In a large mixing bowl place half of the cake mix along with the oil, egg, and orange zest. Blend with an electric mixer set on medium-high speed 1–2 minutes, until blended and smooth. Stir in the remaining cake mix with a wooden spoon until all dry ingredients are moistened.

Gently fold in the chopped mandarin oranges.

Drop dough by teaspoonfuls, 2 inches apart, onto prepared cookie sheets.

Bake 9–12 minutes until set at edges and just barely set at center when lightly touched. Cool 1 minute on sheets. Transfer to wire racks with metal spatula and cool completely.

Prepare Orange Icing; drizzle icing over cooled cookies.

Makes about 4 dozen cookies.

Kahlua Cookies

Impressive to serve yet simple to prepare, these caffeinated cookies are definitely for adults. The type of chocolate chip chosen really makes a difference in the result. Semisweet chips make for a European-tasting cookie (consider adding ½ teaspoon ground cinnamon), milk chocolate chips an American-style mocha flavor, and white chocolate chips create a coffee & cream cookie.

⅓	cup Kahlua or other coffee liqueur
2	teaspoons instant coffee or espresso powder
1	18.25-ounce package vanilla cake mix
¼	cup (½ stick) butter, melted
1	large egg
1¼	cups semisweet, milk, or white chocolate chips

Preheat oven to 350°. Position oven rack in middle of oven. Spray cookie sheets with nonstick cooking spray.

In a large mixing bowl mix the Kahlua and coffee powder until blended. To the same bowl add half of the cake mix along with the melted butter and egg. Blend with an electric mixer set on medium-high speed 1–2 minutes, until blended and smooth. Stir in the remaining cake mix and chocolate chips with a wooden spoon until all dry ingredients are moistened.

Drop dough by teaspoonfuls, 2 inches apart, onto prepared cookie sheets.

Bake 10–13 minutes until set at edges and just barely set at center when lightly touched. Cool 1 minute on sheets. Transfer to wire racks with metal spatula and cool completely.

Makes about 4 dozen cookies.

Orange Chocolate-Chip Cream Cheese Drops

Here's a cookie with a delicate, tender texture and a subtle tang. Both qualities are owed to the addition of cream cheese to the dough—it's a fine foil for the dark, miniature chocolate chips scattered throughout. Lemon zest may be interchanged for the orange zest with equal success.

1   **18.25-ounce package vanilla cake mix**
¼   **cup (½ stick) butter, melted**
1   **8-ounce package cream cheese, softened**
1   **large egg**
1   **tablespoon grated orange zest**
1   **cup miniature semisweet chocolate chips**

Preheat oven to 350°. Position oven rack in middle of oven.

In a large mixing bowl place half of the cake mix along with the melted butter, softened cream cheese, egg, and orange zest. Blend with an electric mixer set on medium-high speed 1–2 minutes, until blended and smooth. Stir in the remaining cake mix and miniature chocolate chips with a wooden spoon until all dry ingredients are moistened.

Drop dough by teaspoonfuls, 2 inches apart, onto ungreased cookie sheets.

Bake 9–12 minutes or until set at edges and just barely set at center when lightly touched (do not overbake; cookies will become more firm as they cool). Transfer to wire rack and cool completely.

Makes about 4 dozen cookies.

Apricot Chews

Apricot fans rejoice—this is an exceptional cookie,
chewy and rich with fruit.

1	8-ounce package cream cheese, softened
¼	cup (½ stick) butter, softened
1	large egg yolk
2	tablespoons milk
1	tablespoon grated orange zest
1	18.25-ounce package vanilla cake mix
1	cup chopped dried apricots
½	cup sweetened flaked coconut

Preheat oven to 350°. Position oven rack in middle of oven.

In a large bowl beat the softened cream cheese and butter with an electric mixer set on low speed until blended and smooth. Beat in egg yolk, milk and orange zest. Beat in half of the cake mix until well blended. Stir in remaining cake mix, apricots, and coconut with a wooden spoon.

Drop dough by rounded teaspoonfuls, 2 inches apart, onto ungreased cookie sheets.

Bake 10–12 minutes or until just set and bottoms of cookies are lightly browned. Remove cookies to wire racks to cool completely.

Makes about 4½ dozen cookies.

Black Forest Oatmeal Cookies

The combination of chocolate and cherry is always a crowd pleaser, which is why these easily assembled cookies are a guaranteed hit. Be sure to make an extra batch during the holiday season—a plateful will only last so long.

1	18.25-ounce package devil's food cake mix
½	cup vegetable oil
2	large eggs
½	teaspoon almond extract
1	cup quick-cooking oats
1	cup miniature semisweet chocolate chips
1	cup tart dried cherries (or dried cranberries)

Preheat oven to 375°. Position oven rack in middle of oven. Spray cookie sheets with nonstick cooking spray.

In a large mixing bowl place half of the cake mix along with the oil, eggs, and almond extract. Blend with an electric mixer set on medium-high speed 1–2 minutes, until blended and smooth. Stir in the remaining cake mix, oats, miniature chocolate chips, and dried cherries with a wooden spoon until all dry ingredients are moistened (dough will be stiff).

Drop dough by heaping teaspoonfuls, 2 inches apart, onto prepared cookie sheets.

Bake 9–12 minutes or until set at edges and just barely set at center when lightly touched (do not overbake). Cool 1 minute on sheets. Transfer to wire racks with metal spatula and cool completely.

Makes about 4 dozen cookies.

Cashew Brickle Cookies

Toffee fans beware; these cookies are highly addictive. Other roasted nuts may be substituted, but buttery cashews make for a very special confection.

1   18.25-ounce package vanilla cake mix
½   cup (1 stick) butter, melted
3   tablespoons dark brown sugar
2   large eggs
⅔   cup quick-cooking oats
1   cup coarsely chopped, lightly salted roasted cashews
¾   cup English toffee baking bits

Preheat oven to 350°. Position oven rack in middle of oven.

In a large mixing bowl mix the cake mix, melted butter, brown sugar, eggs, oats, cashews, and toffee bits with a wooden spoon until all dry ingredients are moistened.

Drop by teaspoonfuls, 2 inches apart, onto ungreased cookie sheets.

Bake 10–13 minutes or until cracked in appearance and just barely set at center when lightly touched. Cool 1 minute on sheets. Transfer to wire racks with metal spatula and cool completely.

Makes about 4½ dozen cookies.

Dried Apple Cider Cookies

While fresh apples lead to soft, sometimes cake-like cookies,
dried apples create a slightly chewy, toothsome treat.
The apple flavor is intensified here with apple cider.
All in all, it's a cookie that epitomizes autumn.

1	18.25-ounce package yellow cake mix
¼	cup apple cider (or apple juice)
¼	cup vegetable oil
½	teaspoon ground cinnamon
1	large egg
1⅓	cups chopped dried apples
1¼	cups chopped walnuts, optional

Preheat oven to 350°. Position oven rack in middle of oven. Spray cookie sheets with nonstick cooking spray.

In a large mixing bowl place half of the cake mix along with the apple cider, oil, cinnamon, and egg. Blend with an electric mixer set on medium-high speed 1–2 minutes, until blended and smooth. Stir in the remaining cake mix and dried apples with a wooden spoon until all dry ingredients are moistened.

Drop dough by teaspoonfuls, 2 inches apart, onto prepared cookie sheets. If desired, sprinkle cookie tops with chopped nuts; gently press nuts into dough.

Bake 10–13 minutes or until set at edges and just barely set at center when lightly touched. Cool 1 minute on sheets. Transfer to wire racks with metal spatula and cool completely.

Makes about 4 dozen cookies.

Mint Julep Cookies

The arrival of spring brings both the Kentucky Derby and the mint julep, a very elegant, very potent potion made of bourbon and fresh mint. Here the libation takes cookie form in a quick, but equally elegant cookie. Be warned—they're potent!

1	**18.25-ounce package vanilla cake mix**
⅓	**cup bourbon (or whiskey)**
¼	**cup (½ stick) butter, melted**
¾	**teaspoon peppermint extract**
1	**large egg**
1	**6-ounce white chocolate baking bar, chopped**

Preheat oven to 350°. Spray cookie sheets with nonstick cooking spray.

In a large mixing bowl place half of the cake mix along with the bourbon, melted butter, peppermint extract, and egg. Blend with an electric mixer set on medium-high speed 1–2 minutes, until blended and smooth. Stir in the remaining cake mix and chopped white chocolate with a wooden spoon until all dry ingredients are moistened.

Drop dough by teaspoonfuls, 2 inches apart, onto prepared cookie sheets.

Bake 10–13 minutes or until set at edges and just barely set at center when lightly touched. Cool 1 minute on sheets. Transfer to wire racks with metal spatula and cool completely.

Variation:

Bittersweet Chocolate Mint Julep Cookies: Prepare as directed above but substitute chocolate cake mix for the vanilla cake mix and 6 ounces bittersweet baking chocolate for the white chocolate.

Makes about 4 dozen cookies.

Bananarama Softies

How is it that such simple foods, like these soft, nutmeg-scented banana cookies, have such wide appeal? My guess is that it's because, like many favorite things, the familiar comforts are what we like best.

1	medium, ripe banana
1	large egg
2	tablespoons vegetable oil
1	18.25-ounce package yellow cake mix
½	teaspoon ground nutmeg
1	cup chopped walnuts (or pecans), optional

Preheat oven to 350°. Position oven rack in middle of oven. Spray cookie sheets with nonstick cooking spray.

In a large mixing bowl mash the banana. Add the egg, oil, half of the cake mix, and the nutmeg. Blend with an electric mixer set on medium-high speed 1–2 minutes, until blended and smooth. Stir in the remaining cake mix with a wooden spoon until all dry ingredients are moistened.

Drop by teaspoonfuls, 2 inches apart, onto prepared cookie sheets. If desired, sprinkle tops of cookies with chopped nuts; gently press nuts into dough.

Bake 10–13 minutes or until set at edges and just barely set at center when lightly touched (do not overbake). Cool 1 minute on sheets. Transfer to wire racks with metal spatula and cool completely.

Makes about 4 dozen cookies.

Pumpkin Spice Softies

*Rediscover a family favorite—in minutes—with this quickly assembled
cookie. They keep well—that is, if you can keep them from being gobbled up.*

1   **18.25-ounce package spice cake mix**
⅔   **cup canned pumpkin purée**
1   **large egg**
2   **tablespoons vegetable oil**
1   **teaspoon pumpkin pie spice**
1   **cup raisins (or dried cranberries), optional**
1   **recipe Vanilla Icing (see page 216), optional**

Preheat oven to 350°. Position oven rack in middle of oven. Spray cookie sheets with nonstick cooking spray.

In a large mixing bowl place half of the cake mix along with the pumpkin, egg, oil, and pumpkin pie spice. Blend with an electric mixer set on medium-high speed 1–2 minutes, until blended and smooth. Stir in the remaining cake mix and optional raisins with a wooden spoon until all dry ingredients are moistened.

Drop by teaspoonfuls, 2 inches apart, onto prepared cookie sheets. If desired, sprinkle tops of cookies with chopped nuts; gently press nuts into dough.

Bake 10–13 minutes or until set at edges and just barely set at center when lightly touched (do not overbake). Cool 1 minute on sheets. Transfer to wire racks with metal spatula and cool completely. If desired, drizzle with Vanilla Icing.

Makes about 4 dozen cookies.

Texas-sized Red Velvet Softies with Cream Cheese Frosting

Texas-sized indeed—these great big, bright red cookies are more like little cakes than cookies. As big as they are, most people will still want more than one.

1   **cup jarred applesauce**
⅓   **cup butter, softened**
1   **18.25-ounce package red velvet cake mix**
2   **large eggs**
½   **cup milk**
1   **recipe Cream Cheese Frosting (see page 212)**

Preheat oven to 375°. Position oven rack in middle of oven. Line a cookie sheet with parchment paper or foil (grease foil, if using).

In a large mixing bowl beat applesauce and softened butter with an electric mixer on medium speed until smooth. Add cake mix, eggs, and milk; beat on low speed until combined and then on medium speed for 1 minute. By heaping tablespoonfuls, drop mounds of batter, 3 inches apart, onto prepared cookie sheet; keep remaining batter chilled.

Bake 15 minutes or until set and lightly browned around edges.

Carefully remove from parchment or foil; cool on wire rack. Repeat with remaining batter, lining cooled cookie sheets each time with new parchment or foil. If desired, place cookies in a covered storage container with waxed paper between layers to prevent sticking.

Prepare Cream Cheese Icing. Frost the cookies.

Makes about 2½ dozen big cookies.

Coconut, Cashew, & White Chocolate Chewies

Newfangled has never been better than with this delectable cookie.
Crunchy cashews, chewy coconut, butter, and white chocolate?
Hooray for innovation!

¼ cup butter, softened
1 8-ounce package cream cheese, softened
1 14-ounce can sweetened condensed milk
1 large egg
2 teaspoons vanilla extract
1 cup all-purpose flour
1 18.25-ounce package yellow cake mix
1½ cups coarsely chopped, lightly salted roasted cashews
1⅓ cups shredded coconut
1½ cups white chocolate chips

Preheat oven to 375°. Position oven rack in middle of oven. Spray cookie sheets with nonstick cooking spray.

In a large mixing bowl beat butter and cream cheese with electric mixer set on high until smooth. Add sweetened condensed milk, egg, and vanilla extract; beat until blended. Add flour and cake mix; stir with wooden spoon until blended and all dry ingredients are moistened. Stir in cashews, coconut, and white chocolate chips.

Drop dough by teaspoonfuls, 1 inch apart, onto prepared cookie sheets.

Bake 9–12 minutes or until set at edges and just barely set at center when lightly touched. Cool 1 minute on sheets. Transfer to wire racks with metal spatula and cool completely.

Makes about 5 dozen cookies.

Lemon-Ginger
Cream Cheese Softies

*The pleasant bite of ginger coupled with the zing of lemon gives
these cookies grown-up appeal.*

1	18.25-ounce package lemon cake mix
2	teaspoons ground ginger
¼	cup (½ stick) butter, melted
4	ounces (half of an 8-ounce package) cream cheese, softened
1	large egg
1	recipe Lemon Icing (see page 213), optional

Preheat oven to 350°. Position oven rack in middle of oven.

In a large mixing bowl place half of the cake mix along with the ginger, melted butter, softened cream cheese, and egg. Blend with an electric mixer set on medium-high speed 1–2 minutes, until blended and smooth. Stir in the remaining cake mix with a wooden spoon until all dry ingredients are moistened (dough will be sticky).

Drop dough by teaspoonfuls, 2 inches apart, onto ungreased cookie sheets; smooth edge of each to form round cookie.

Bake 9–12 minutes or until edges are set and just barely set at center when lightly touched (do not overbake; cookies will become more firm as they cool). Transfer to wire rack and cool completely. If desired, prepare lemon icing; drizzle over cooled cookies.

Makes 4 dozen cookies.

Jumbo Jumble Chocolate Oatmeal Cookies

When the kitchen is warm from baking and the cookie jar is full with these everything-but-the-kitchen-sink chocolate cookies, who cares if it's cold outside?

1   18.25-ounce package chocolate or devil's food cake mix
1   cup vegetable oil
3   large eggs
2   cups quick-cooking oats
1   cup semisweet or milk chocolate chips
1   cup miniature candy-coated chocolate baking pieces (e.g., baking M&Ms)
½   cup raisins (or dried cranberries)

In a large mixing bowl place the cake mix, oil, and eggs. Blend with an electric mixer set on medium-high speed 1–2 minutes, until blended and smooth. Stir in the oats, chocolate chips, baking pieces, and raisins with a wooden spoon until well blended. Let stand 30 minutes (oats will absorb some of the liquid).

Preheat oven to 350°. Position oven rack in middle of oven. Spray cookie sheets with nonstick cooking spray.

Drop dough by level ¼-cupfuls, 2 inches apart, onto prepared cookie sheets; flatten slightly with the bottom of a glass.

Bake 13–17 minutes or until set at edges and just barely set at center when lightly touched. Cool 1 minute on sheets. Transfer to wire racks with metal spatula and cool completely.

Makes 2 dozen big cookies.

Caramel Apple Cookies

In general, and as a guiding rule, tamper with tradition and that wonderful thing called nostalgia only up to a certain point. Case in point, these cookies, which showcase all the best flavors of classic caramel apples but in convenient cookie form.

2   1.7-ounce packages chewy chocolate-covered caramel candies (e.g., Rolos®), unwrapped and quartered
1   18.25-ounce package yellow cake mix
½   cup vegetable oil
¼   cup packed light brown sugar
2   large eggs
1   teaspoon vanilla extract
1   6-ounce package dried apples, chopped

Preheat oven to 350°. Position oven rack in middle of oven.

In a small bowl toss the chopped candies with 2 tablespoons of the cake mix (to prevent sticking).

In a large mixing bowl place half of the cake mix along with the oil, brown sugar, eggs, and vanilla extract. Blend with an electric mixer set on medium-high speed 1–2 minutes, until blended and smooth. Stir in the remaining cake mix, caramel candies, and dried apples with a wooden spoon until all dry ingredients are moistened.

Drop by teaspoonfuls, 2 inches apart, onto ungreased cookie sheets.

Bake 10–13 minutes or until just barely set at center when lightly touched. Cool 2 minutes on sheets. Transfer to wire racks with metal spatula and cool completely.

Makes about 4 ½ dozen cookies.

Cinnamon-Chip Chews

When a magic wand—or, perhaps, a magic cinnamon stick—is waved over classic chocolate-chip cookies, this is the sweet and spicy result. Cinnamon chips can be found in the baking aisle of the supermarket alongside chocolate chips. They look and melt like chocolate chips (although tan in color) and are a cinnamon lover's delight.

1   18.25-ounce package spice cake mix
⅓   cup water
¼   cup (½ stick) butter, melted
1   large egg
1   teaspoon ground cinnamon
1½   cups cinnamon baking chips

Preheat oven to 350°. Position oven rack in middle of oven. Spray cookie sheets with nonstick cooking spray.

In a large mixing bowl place half of the cake mix along with the water, melted butter, egg, and cinnamon. Blend with an electric mixer set on medium-high speed 1–2 minutes, until blended and smooth. Stir in the remaining cake mix and cinnamon chips with a wooden spoon until all dry ingredients are moistened.

Drop dough by teaspoonfuls, 2 inches apart, onto prepared cookie sheets.

Bake 9–12 minutes or until set at edges and just barely set at center when lightly touched. Cool 1 minute on sheets. Transfer to wire racks with metal spatula and cool completely.

Makes about 4 dozen cookies.

Ranger Cookies

Chock-full of everything, ranger cookies are old-time favorites, and with good reason: they taste like home, keep well, and are great travelers for lunch boxes and picnics. Make a batch and there's just one thing left to do—sit, eat, and enjoy.

1	18.25-ounce package yellow cake mix
¾	cup vegetable oil
⅓	cup chunky peanut butter (not old-fashioned or natural style)
3	large eggs
1½	cups quick-cooking oats
⅔	cup semisweet chocolate chips, raisins, or dried cranberries
½	cup sweetened flaked coconut

Preheat oven to 350°. Position oven rack in middle of oven.

In a large mixing bowl place the cake mix, oil, peanut butter, and eggs. Blend with an electric mixer set on medium-high speed 1–2 minutes, until blended and smooth. Stir in the oats, chocolate chips (or dried fruit), and coconut with a wooden spoon until all dry ingredients are moistened (dough will be very stiff).

Drop dough by level ¼-cupfuls, 2 inches apart, onto ungreased cookie sheets; flatten slightly with the bottom of a glass.

Bake 13–17 minutes or until set at edges and just barely set at center when lightly touched. Cool 1 minute on sheets. Transfer to wire racks with metal spatula and cool completely.

Makes 2½ dozen big cookies.

Old-fashioned Hermits

Hermits—spicy drop cookies filled with fruits and nuts—have been filling American cookie jars since colonial times. Here they are better than ever—and simplified with the help of cake mix.

1   **18.25-ounce package spice cake mix**
1   **teaspoon pumpkin pie spice**
⅓   **cup butter, softened**
1   **3-ounce package cream cheese, softened**
2   **large eggs**
1   **tablespoon grated orange zest**
1   **cup snipped dates, raisins, or currants**
1   **cup chopped walnuts (or pecans)**

Preheat oven to 350°. Position oven rack in middle of oven. Spray cookie sheets with nonstick cooking spray.

In a large mixing bowl place half of the cake mix along with the pumpkin pie spice, softened butter, softened cream cheese, eggs, and orange zest. Blend with an electric mixer set on medium-high speed 1–2 minutes, until blended and smooth. Stir in the remaining cake mix and dried fruit with a wooden spoon until all dry ingredients are moistened.

Drop by teaspoonfuls, 2 inches apart, onto prepared cookie sheets. Sprinkle tops with nuts.

Bake 9–12 minutes or until firm at edges and center is just barely set when lightly touched. Cool 1 minute on sheets. Transfer to wire racks with metal spatula and cool completely.

Makes about 4 ½ dozen cookies.

Applesauce Cookies

*This slightly spicy, nostalgic cookie is simple and good,
with lots of familiar flavors and a soft, old-fashioned texture—just
what you want to bake on a cool autumn day.*

1	18.25-ounce package spice cake mix
½	cup vegetable oil
½	cup applesauce
1	large egg
1	cup raisins (or dried cranberries)

Preheat oven to 350F. Position oven rack in middle of oven. Spray cookie sheets with nonstick cooking spray.

In a large mixing bowl place the cake mix, oil, applesauce, and egg. Blend with an electric mixer set on medium-high speed 1–2 minutes, until blended and smooth. Stir in the raisins or dried cranberries.

Drop by teaspoonfuls, 2 inches apart, onto prepared cookie sheets.

Bake 9–12 minutes or until edges are firm and center is just barely set when lightly touched. Cool 1 minute on sheets. Transfer to wire racks with metal spatula and cool completely.

Makes about 4 dozen cookies.

Ginger-jeweled Butter Cookies

*These cookies warrant singular attention. When you taste them—
rich with butter, bejeweled with bits of peppery, candied ginger—you
will understand why. Don't forget the pot of strong Indian black tea.*

1   **18.25-ounce package yellow cake mix**
⅓   **cup butter, softened**
1   **large egg**
1   **teaspoon ground ginger**
⅔   **cup chopped crystallized ginger**

Preheat oven to 350°. Position oven rack in middle of oven.

In a large mixing bowl place half of the cake mix along with the softened butter, egg, and ginger. Blend with an electric mixer set on medium-high speed 1–2 minutes, until blended and smooth. Stir in the remaining cake mix and crystallized ginger with a wooden spoon until all dry ingredients are moistened.

Drop by teaspoonfuls, 2 inches apart, onto ungreased cookie sheets.

Bake 9–12 minutes or until edges are firm and center is just barely set at center when lightly touched. Cool 1 minute on sheets. Transfer to wire racks with metal spatula and cool completely.

Makes about 4 dozen cookies.

TWO

Bar Cookies

Chocolate-Chip Toffee Bars

Toffee bar recipes are relatively easy to come by. Exceptional toffee bars, on the other hand, are an entirely different matter. For example, this recipe. Decadent with nuts, toffee, and chocolate but still easy to assemble—one bite and I think you'll decide this is the only toffee bar recipe you'll need from now on.

1   18.25-ounce package yellow cake mix
½   cup (1 stick) butter, softened
1   large egg
1   cup coarsely chopped nuts (e.g., walnuts, pecans, or peanuts)
2   cups semisweet chocolate chips, divided
1   14-ounce can sweetened condensed milk
1   10-ounce package toffee baking bits, divided

Preheat oven to 350° (or 325° for dark-coated metal pan). Position oven rack in middle of oven. Spray the bottom only of a 13 x 9-inch metal baking pan with nonstick cooking spray (or foil-line pan; see page 11).

In a large bowl mix cake mix, softened butter, and egg with an electric mixer set on medium speed until blended and crumbly; stir in nuts and 1½ cups chocolate chips. Set aside 1½ cups of the crumb mixture. Firmly press remaining crumb mixture into bottom of prepared pan.

Bake 15 minutes.

Pour condensed milk evenly over partially baked crust; top with 1½ cups of the toffee bits. Sprinkle the reserved crumb mixture and remaining ½ cup chocolate chips evenly over top.

Bake 25–28 minutes or until golden brown. Immediately sprinkle with remaining ¼ cup toffee bits. Transfer to wire rack and cool completely. Cut into bars.

Variations:
Double Chocolate Toffee Bars: Prepare as directed above but use chocolate cake mix in place of the yellow cake mix.

Best Butterscotch Bars: Prepare as directed above but use pecans for the nuts and use butterscotch baking chips in place of the chocolate chips.

Chocolate-Chip Toffee Bars

Makes 24 large or 36 small bars.

Rocky Road Bars

A lumpy-bumpy cookie made of marshmallow, chocolate, and nuts?
Who wouldn't want to take a stroll down rocky road?

1   18.25-ounce package chocolate or devil's food cake mix
½   cup (1 stick) butter, melted
¼   cup water
2   large eggs
3   cups miniature marshmallows
1   cup roasted peanuts (or cashews)
1   cup semisweet or milk chocolate chips

Preheat oven to 350° (or 325° for dark-coated metal pan). Position oven rack in middle of oven. Spray the bottom only of a 13 x 9-inch metal baking pan with nonstick cooking spray (or foil-line pan; see page 11).

In a large bowl mix cake mix along with the melted butter, water, and eggs with an electric mixer set on medium speed 1–2 minutes, until well blended and all dry ingredients are moistened. Spread mixture evenly in prepared pan.

Bake 25 minutes. Remove from oven and sprinkle with marshmallows, nuts, and chocolate chips.

Bake 5–8 minutes longer or until marshmallows are puffed and golden. Transfer to wire rack and cool completely. Cut into bars.

Makes 24 large or 36 small bars.

Cherry Pie Bars

Come cherry season, it's hard to escape the allure of the sweet little fruits. But if the notion of baking a pie seems like too much work, consider these simple bars, which offer the pleasure of pie with a lot less effort.

1	18.25-ounce package vanilla cake mix
8	tablespoons (1 stick) butter, melted, divided
1¼	cups quick-cooking oats, divided
1	large egg
1	21-ounce can cherry pie filling
¼	cup packed light brown sugar
½	cup chopped pecans

Preheat oven to 350° (or 325° for dark-coated metal pan). Position oven rack in middle of oven. Spray the bottom only of a 13 x 9-inch metal baking pan with nonstick cooking spray (or foil-line pan; see page 11).

In large bowl mix cake mix, 6 tablespoons melted butter, and 1 cup of the oats with a wooden spoon until well blended (mixture will be crumbly); reserve 1 cup of crumb mixture. Stir the egg into the remaining mixture until well blended; press into bottom of prepared pan.

Pour cherry pie filling over crust. In small bowl combine reserved cake mixture, remaining ¼ cup oats, remaining 2 tablespoons melted butter, brown sugar, and pecans until blended; sprinkle evenly over cherry filling.

Bake 30–35 minutes or until filling is bubbly and topping is golden. Transfer to wire rack and cool completely. Cut into bars.

Variation:

Chocolate Cherry Pie Bars: Prepare as directed above but use chocolate cake mix in place of vanilla cake mix and use 1 cup miniature semisweet chocolate chips in place of the pecans.

Makes 24 large or 36 small bars.

Chocolate Caramel Peanut Butter Bars

If ever there was a pull-out-all-the-stops bar cookie, this is it. Caramel, chocolate, cream cheese, peanut butter—on a scale of 1–10, these are an 11.

1   18.25-ounce package white cake mix
1   cup quick-cooking oats
½   cup creamy-style peanut butter
1   large egg
2   tablespoons milk
1   8-ounce package cream cheese, softened
1   12-ounce jar caramel ice cream topping
2   cups milk or semisweet chocolate chips
1   cup cocktail peanuts

Preheat oven to 350° (or 325° for dark-coated metal pan). Position oven rack in middle of oven. Spray the bottom only of a 13 x 9-inch metal baking pan with nonstick cooking spray (or foil-line pan; see page 11).

In a large bowl mix the cake mix and oats. Using your fingers or a pastry blender, cut in the peanut butter until mixture resembles fine crumbs. In a small cup beat the egg with the milk; add to the oat mixture, stirring until well blended. Reserve 1 cup of the oat mixture; press remaining mixture into bottom of prepared pan.

In a medium bowl beat the cream cheese with an electric mixer set on medium speed until blended and smooth. Add caramel topping; beat until blended and smooth. Spread cream cheese mixture on top of prepared crust. Sprinkle evenly with chocolate chips and peanuts to cover. Sprinkle evenly with reserved oat mixture.

Bake 28–30 minutes until topping is golden. Transfer to wire rack and cool completely. Cut into bars.

Makes 24 large or 36 small bars.

Cranberry Caramel Bars

Spectacular but easy, thanks to boxed cake mix and canned cranberry sauce.

1	14-ounce package caramels, unwrapped
⅔	cup half & half (light cream), divided
1	18.25-ounce package white cake mix
¼	cup (½ stick) butter, melted
1	teaspoon vanilla extract
1	16-ounce can whole cranberry sauce, stirred to loosen
½	cup chopped pecans

Preheat oven to 350° (or 325° for dark-coated metal pan). Position oven rack in middle of oven. Spray the bottom only of a 13 x 9-inch metal baking pan with nonstick cooking spray (or foil-line pan; see page 11).

In a heavy medium saucepan set over low heat melt caramels with ⅓ cup of the cream, stirring until melted and smooth. Remove from heat and set aside momentarily.

Meanwhile, in a large bowl beat cake mix, remaining ⅓ cup cream, melted butter, and vanilla extract with an electric mixer set on medium speed 1–2 minutes, until blended. Pat half of the mixture into the bottom of prepared pan.

Bake crust 10 minutes; remove from oven. Immediately spread with warm caramel mixture. Spoon cranberry sauce over caramel layer. Dot remaining cake mixture over cranberry layer; sprinkle with the chopped pecans.

Bake bars 25–27 minutes or until topping is firm and deep golden. Transfer to wire rack and cool completely. Cut into bars.

Makes 24 large or 36 small bars.

Dark Chocolate Bars with White Chocolate Raspberry Filling

Scrumptious. These decadent, double chocolate, raspberry-rich bars answer the question of what to make when you want to impress a crowd.

1   18.25-ounce package chocolate cake mix
¼   cup (½ stick) butter, melted
1   large egg
2   cups white chocolate chips, divided
1   14-ounce can sweetened condensed milk
¼   teaspoon almond extract
½   cup chopped walnuts (or pecans)
½   cup seedless raspberry jam

Preheat oven to 350° (or 325° for dark-coated metal pan). Position oven rack in middle of oven. Spray the bottom only of a 13 x 9-inch metal baking pan with nonstick cooking spray (or foil-line pan; see page 11).

In a large bowl place the cake mix, melted butter, and egg. Blend with an electric mixer set on medium speed until crumbly. Set aside 1 cup of the crumb mixture. Firmly press remaining crumb mixture into bottom of prepared pan.

Bake 15 minutes.

In a medium saucepan combine 1 cup white chocolate chips and condensed milk. Warm over low heat, stirring until smooth. Remove from heat and stir in almond extract; spread over hot crust.

Stir nuts into reserved crumb mixture; sprinkle over chocolate filling. Drop teaspoonfuls of raspberry jam over crumb mixture. Sprinkle with remaining white chocolate chips.

Bake 25–28 minutes or until topping is firm to the touch. Transfer to wire rack and cool completely. Cut into bars.

Makes 24 large or 36 small bars.

Dark Chocolate Bars with White Chocolate Raspberry Filling

Caramel Mallow Butterscotch Bars

We all know about the great matches that chocolate & peanut butter, lemon & ginger and cinnamon & vanilla make. Well, here's another made-for-each-other combination: caramel and marshmallow. Prepare to hoot and holler when you take a bite.

1	18.25-ounce package yellow cake mix
¼	cup (1 stick) butter, melted
¼	cup water
¼	cup packed light brown sugar
2	large eggs
3	cups miniature marshmallows
1	cup butterscotch baking chips
¾	cup caramel ice cream topping

Preheat oven to 350° (or 325° for dark-coated metal pan). Position oven rack in middle of oven. Spray the bottom only of a 13 x 9-inch metal baking pan with nonstick cooking spray (or foil-line pan; see page 11).

In a large bowl place cake mix, melted butter, water, brown sugar, and eggs. Blend with an electric mixer 1–2 minutes on medium speed, until well blended and crumbly. Press mixture evenly in prepared pan.

Bake 15–18 minutes or until golden. Remove from oven and sprinkle with marshmallows and butterscotch baking chips.

Bake 5–8 minutes longer or until marshmallows are puffed and golden. Transfer to wire rack and cool completely. Drizzle with caramel topping. Cut into bars.

Makes 24 large or 36 small bars.

Chocolate Truffle Crumb Bars

An opulent treat for chocolate lovers, this recipe involves a rich chocolate truffle filling sandwiched between two layers of chocolate streusel to create a uniquely delicious chocolate treat.

1   18.25-ounce package chocolate cake mix
⅓   cup butter, melted
1   large egg
2   cups semisweet chocolate chips, divided
1   14-ounce can sweetened condensed milk
2   teaspoons vanilla extract
1   cup chopped walnuts

Preheat oven to 350° (or 325° for dark-coated metal pan). Position oven rack in middle of oven. Spray the bottom only of a 13 x 9-inch metal baking pan with nonstick cooking spray (or foil-line pan; see page 11).

In large bowl place the cake mix, melted butter, and egg. Blend 1–2 minutes with an electric mixer set on medium speed until crumbly. Set aside 1 cup of the crumb mixture. Firmly press remaining crumb mixture into bottom of prepared 13 x 9-inch baking pan.

Bake 15 minutes.

In a medium saucepan combine 1 cup of the chocolate chips and condensed milk. Warm over low heat, stirring until smooth. Remove from heat and stir in vanilla; spread over hot crust.

Stir walnuts and remaining 1 cup chocolate chips into reserved crumb mixture; sprinkle over chocolate filling.

Bake 25–28 minutes or until topping is firm to the touch. Transfer to wire rack and cool completely. Cut into bars.

Makes 24 large or 36 small bars.

Chocolate Raspberry Linzer Bars

These intensely chocolate bars are a long way from their Austrian forebears, marrying traditional sense with modern sensibility.

1	18.25-ounce package chocolate cake mix
1	cup finely chopped almonds
⅓	cup vegetable oil
1	large egg
1	teaspoon almond extract
1	12-ounce jar seedless raspberry preserves
1	cup miniature chocolate chips

Preheat oven to 350° (or 325° for dark-coated metal pan). Position oven rack in middle of oven. Spray the bottom only of a 13x9-inch metal baking pan with nonstick cooking spray (or foil-line pan; see page 11).

In a large bowl place cake mix, almonds, oil, egg, and almond extract. Blend with an electric mixer set on medium speed until blended and crumbly. Set aside 1½ cups of the crumb mixture. Firmly press remaining crumb mixture into bottom of prepared pan.

Spread raspberry preserves evenly over crust. Sprinkle with reserved crumb mixture and miniature chocolate chips; gently press into filling layer.

Bake 25–28 minutes or until topping is firm to the touch. Transfer to wire rack and cool completely. Cut into bars.

Variations:

Classic Linzer Bars: Prepare as directed above but use vanilla cake mix in place of chocolate cake mix and eliminate the chocolate chips.

Sacher Torte Bars: Prepare as directed above but use apricot preserves in place of the raspberry preserves.

Makes 24 large or 36 small bars.

Magic Cookie Bars

Call them hello dollies, 7-layer bars, or magic cookie bars—an incredible cookie, no matter the name, tastes just as sweet. A bit of crispy from the toasted coconut and pecans, a touch of buttery from the quick crust, and a good dose of gooey from the condensed milk and chocolate chips guarantee that these will magically disappear from the cookie jar.

1   18.25-ounce package yellow cake mix with pudding in the mix
½   cup (1 stick) butter, softened
2   cups semisweet chocolate chips
1½ cups sweetened flaked coconut
1   cup chopped walnuts (or pecans)
1   14-ounce can sweetened condensed milk

Preheat oven to 350° (or 325° for dark-coated metal pan). Position oven rack in middle of oven.

Place the cake mix and softened butter in a large bowl. Blend 1–2 minutes with an electric mixer set on medium speed until blended and crumbly. Press mixture into a 15 x 10 x 1-inch jelly roll pan.

Sprinkle the crust with the chocolate chips, coconut, and nuts. Pour condensed milk evenly over crust and ingredients.

Bake 25–28 minutes or until lightly browned. Transfer to wire rack. Cool completely. Cut into bars.

Variations:

Butterscotch Magic Cookie Bars: Prepare as directed above but use butterscotch baking chips in place of the chocolate chips.

Double Chocolate Magic Cookie Bars: Prepare as directed above but use chocolate cake mix in place of the yellow cake mix.

Vanilla Magic Cookie Bars: Prepare as directed above but use vanilla cake mix in place of the yellow cake mix, vanilla baking chips or white chocolate chips in place of the semisweet chocolate chips, and sliced almonds in place of the chopped walnuts or pecans.

Makes 48 small bars.

Maui Wowie Magic Bars

For an imaginative cookie, try this aloha-inspired variation on magic cookie bars. They are definitely summer barbecue fare, so invite the guests and fire up the grill.

1	18.25-ounce package yellow cake mix with pudding in the mix
1½	teaspoons ground ginger
½	cup (1 stick) butter, softened
1	14-ounce can sweetened condensed milk
1	tablespoon lime juice
2	teaspoons grated lime zest
1½	cups white chocolate chips
1½	cups sweetened flaked coconut
1	cup chopped macadamia nuts
½	cup pineapple preserves

Preheat oven to 350° (or 325° for dark-coated metal pan). Position oven rack in middle of oven.

In a large bowl place the cake mix, ginger, and softened butter. Blend 1–2 minutes with an electric mixer set on medium speed, until blended and crumbly. Press mixture into a 15 x 10 x 1-inch jelly roll pan.

In a small bowl mix the condensed milk with the lime juice and lime zest. Sprinkle the crust with the white chocolate chips, coconut, and macadamia nuts. Pour condensed milk mixture evenly over crust and ingredients.

Bake 25–28 minutes or until lightly browned. Transfer to wire rack. Heat preserves in a small saucepan set over low heat until melted; drizzle over baked bars. Cool completely. Cut into bars.

Makes 48 small bars.

Salty-Sweet Peanut Chewy Bars

These easy and very delicious bars bear a strong resemblance to one of my favorite candy bars: PayDay®. Have fun playing around with the cake and chip flavors. Consider chocolate cake mix and chocolate chips or caramel cake mix (harder to find, but worth the hunt) combined with butterscotch or white chocolate chips.

1	18.25-ounce package yellow cake mix
10	tablespoons butter, softened, divided
1	large egg
3	cups miniature marshmallows
⅔	cup light corn syrup
1	10-ounce package peanut butter chips
2	teaspoons vanilla extract
2	cups crisp rice cereal
2	cups salted, roasted peanuts

Preheat oven to 350° (or 325° for dark-coated metal pan). Position oven rack in middle of oven. Spray the bottom only of a 13 x 9-inch metal baking pan with nonstick cooking spray (or foil-line pan; see page 11).

In a large bowl place the cake mix, 6 tablespoons softened butter, and egg. Blend 1–2 minutes with an electric mixer set on medium speed until blended and crumbly. Press mixture evenly into prepared pan.

Bake 12–15 minutes or until golden brown. Remove from oven and sprinkle with marshmallows. Return to oven and bake 1–2 minutes longer, until marshmallows begin to puff. Remove from oven and transfer to cooling rack. Cool.

Meanwhile, in a heavy saucepan set over medium heat combine the remaining 4 tablespoons butter, corn syrup, and peanut butter chips; stir until melted and smooth. Stir in vanilla extract, cereal, and peanuts. Evenly spread mixture over marshmallows; refrigerate at least 1 hour. Cut into bars.

Makes 24 large or 36 small bars.

Buttery Gooey Chess Squares

When your kitchen is filled with the enticing aroma of vanilla and butter, you'll know that weekend baking will never be the same. These delectable treats are made with a buttery cake mix dough on the bottom and a generous layer of more butter, cream cheese, and vanilla on top—irresistible!

1	cup (2 sticks) butter, divided
1	18.25-ounce package yellow cake mix
4	large eggs
1	8-ounce package cream cheese, softened
2	teaspoons vanilla extract
1	16-ounce box powdered sugar

Preheat oven to 350° (or 325° for dark-coated metal pan). Position oven rack in middle of oven. Spray the bottom only of a 13 x 9-inch metal baking pan with nonstick cooking spray (or foil-line pan; see page 11).

Melt ½ cup (1 stick) of the butter in a small saucepan set over low heat. In a large bowl beat the cake mix, melted butter, and 1 egg with an electric mixer set on medium speed until well blended (mixture will come together as a thick dough). Pat the dough evenly into the prepared pan. Set aside momentarily.

Melt the remaining stick of butter in a small saucepan set over low heat. In a large bowl beat the softened cream cheese and vanilla extract with an electric mixer set on medium speed until blended and smooth, scraping down sides of bowl occasionally. Add the melted butter and remaining 3 eggs; blend until smooth. Add the powdered sugar; blend until smooth.

Spread cream cheese mixture over prepared crust. Bake 42–45 minutes (do not overbake; bars should be slightly gooey). Transfer to a wire rack and cool completely. Cut into bars or squares. Cover and store in refrigerator.

Makes 24 large or 36 small bars.

Cookies & Cream Gooey Chess Squares

*Life moves quickly these days, but here's a delicious reason
to slow down: rich and gooey and oh-so-comforting bar cookies,
filled with more chopped creme-filled cookies.
They'll bring everyone to the kitchen.*

1   cup (2 sticks) butter, divided
1   18.25-ounce package chocolate cake mix
4   large eggs
1   8-ounce package cream cheese, softened
1   teaspoon vanilla extract
1   16-ounce box powdered sugar
12   creme-filled chocolate sandwich cookies, coarsely crumbled

Preheat oven to 350° (or 325° for dark-coated metal pan). Position oven rack in middle of oven. Spray the bottom only of a 13 x 9-inch metal baking pan with nonstick cooking spray (or foil-line pan; see page 11).

Melt ½ cup (1 stick) of the butter in a small saucepan set over low heat. In a large bowl beat the cake mix, melted butter, and 1 egg with an electric mixer set on medium speed until well blended (mixture will come together as a thick dough). Pat the dough evenly into the prepared pan. Set aside momentarily.

Melt the remaining stick of butter in a small saucepan set over low heat. In a large bowl beat the softened cream cheese and vanilla extract with an electric mixer set on medium speed until blended and smooth, scraping down sides of bowl occasionally. Add the melted butter and remaining 3 eggs; blend until smooth. Add the powdered sugar; blend until smooth.

Stir in the crumbled cookies.

Spread cream cheese mixture over prepared crust. Bake 42–45 minutes (do not overbake; bars should be slightly gooey). Transfer to a wire rack and cool completely. Cut into bars or squares. Cover and store in refrigerator.

Makes 24 large or 36 small bars.

Cookies & Cream Gooey Chess Squares

Pumpkin Gooey Chess Squares

Bye-bye pumpkin pie—that's what you'll likely croon once you try these out-of-this-world chess squares. Be sure to use pure pumpkin in the filling, not pumpkin pie mix. Both come in a can, but the latter is prespiced and presweetened, which will lead to an overly sweet bar with the wrong consistency.

1	cup (2 sticks) butter, divided
1	18.25-ounce package spice or yellow cake mix
4	large eggs
1	8-ounce package cream cheese, softened
1	15-ounce can pumpkin purée
2	teaspoons vanilla extract
1	16-ounce box powdered sugar
2	teaspoons pumpkin pie spice (or ground cinnamon)

Preheat oven to 350° (or 325° for dark-coated metal pan). Position oven rack in middle of oven. Spray the bottom only of a 13 x 9-inch metal baking pan with nonstick cooking spray (or foil-line pan; see page 11).

Melt ½ cup (1 stick) of the butter in a small saucepan set over low heat. In a large bowl beat the cake mix, melted butter, and 1 egg with an electric mixer set on medium speed until well blended (mixture will come together as a thick dough). Pat the dough evenly into the prepared pan. Set aside momentarily.

Melt the remaining stick of butter in a small saucepan set over low heat. In a large bowl beat the softened cream cheese and pumpkin purée with an electric mixer set on medium speed until blended and smooth, scraping down sides of bowl occasionally. Add the melted butter, remaining 3 eggs and vanilla extract; blend until smooth. Add the powdered sugar and pumpkin pie spice; blend until smooth.

Spread pumpkin mixture over prepared crust. Bake 42–45 minutes (do not overbake; bars should be slightly gooey). Transfer to a wire rack and cool completely. Cut into bars or squares. Cover and store in refrigerator.

Makes 24 large or 36 small bars.

Pineapple Gooey Chess Squares

These sunny, golden bars are chock-full of fruits and flavor: zesty lime, chunks of moist, naturally sweet Hawaiian pineapple, and peppery ginger—all baked to perfection in a rich, buttery batter.

1   cup (2 sticks) butter, divided
1   18.25-ounce package yellow cake mix
4   large eggs
1   8-ounce package cream cheese, softened
1   20-ounce can of crushed pineapple, well drained
2   tablespoons fresh lime juice
1   teaspoon grated lime zest
1   16-ounce box powdered sugar
1½   teaspoons ground ginger

Preheat oven to 350° (or 325° for dark-coated metal pan). Position oven rack in middle of oven. Spray the bottom only of a 13x9-inch metal baking pan with nonstick cooking spray (or foil-line pan; see page 11).

Melt ½ cup (1 stick) of the butter in a small saucepan set over low heat. In a large bowl beat the cake mix, melted butter, and 1 egg with an electric mixer set on medium speed until well blended (mixture will come together as a thick dough). Pat the dough evenly into the prepared pan. Set aside momentarily.

Melt the remaining stick of butter in a small saucepan set over low heat. In a large bowl beat the cream cheese, pineapple, lime juice, and lime zest with an electric mixer set on medium speed until well blended, scraping down sides of bowl occasionally. Add the melted butter and remaining 3 eggs; blend until smooth. Add the powdered sugar and ginger; blend until smooth.

Spread pineapple mixture over prepared crust. Bake 42–45 minutes (do not overbake; bars should be slightly gooey). Transfer to a wire rack and cool completely. Cut into bars or squares. Cover and store in refrigerator.

Makes 24 large or 36 small bars.

Banana Bliss Gooey Chess Squares

Who would have guessed that such commonly available, reasonably priced ingredients—a cake mix, a few bananas and a package of cream cheese—could lead to such a supreme treat, with such little effort to boot? Kids of all ages will line up for seconds (and thirds!).

1   cup (2 sticks) butter, divided
1   18.25-ounce package yellow or chocolate cake mix
4   large eggs
1   8-ounce package cream cheese, softened
1½ cups mashed banana (about 2 large bananas)
2   teaspoons vanilla extract
1   16-ounce box powdered sugar
½   teaspoon ground nutmeg

Preheat oven to 350° (or 325° for dark-coated metal pan). Position oven rack in middle of oven. Spray the bottom only of a 13 x 9-inch metal baking pan with nonstick cooking spray (or foil-line pan; see page 11).

Melt ½ cup (1 stick) of the butter in a small saucepan set over low heat. In a large bowl beat the cake mix, melted butter, and 1 egg with an electric mixer set on medium speed until well blended (mixture will come together as a thick dough). Pat the dough evenly into the prepared pan. Set aside momentarily.

Melt the remaining stick of butter in a small saucepan set over low heat. In a large bowl beat the cream cheese and mashed banana with an electric mixer set on medium speed until blended and smooth, scraping down sides of bowl occasionally. Add the melted butter, remaining 3 eggs, and vanilla extract; blend until smooth. Add the powdered sugar and nutmeg; blend until smooth.

Spread banana mixture over prepared crust. Bake 42–45 minutes (do not overbake; bars should be slightly gooey). Transfer to a wire rack and cool completely. Cut into bars or squares. Cover and store in refrigerator.

Makes 24 large or 36 small bars.

Peanut Butter–Chocolate Gooey Chess Squares

*Holy moly. Yes, the combination of chocolate and peanut butter
is a match made in heaven, but it has never been quite so good
as in these gooey bars. Part cake, part cookie, they are
100 percent scrumptious.*

1   cup (2 sticks) butter, divided
1   18.25-ounce package chocolate cake mix
4   large eggs
1   8-ounce package cream cheese, softened
1   cup creamy-style peanut butter
1   teaspoon vanilla extract
1   16-ounce box powdered sugar

Preheat oven to 350° (or 325° for dark-coated metal pan). Position oven rack in middle of oven. Spray the bottom only of a 13 x 9-inch metal baking pan with nonstick cooking spray (or foil-line pan; see page 11).

Melt ½ cup (1 stick) of the butter in a small saucepan set over low heat. In a large bowl beat the cake mix, melted butter, and 1 egg with an electric mixer set on medium speed until well blended (mixture will come together as a thick dough). Pat the dough evenly into the prepared pan. Set aside momentarily.

Melt the remaining stick of butter in a small saucepan set over low heat. In a large bowl beat the softened cream cheese and peanut butter with an electric mixer set on medium speed until blended and smooth, scraping down sides of bowl occasionally. Add the melted butter, remaining 3 eggs, and vanilla extract; blend until smooth. Add the powdered sugar; blend until smooth.

Spread peanut butter mixture over prepared crust. Bake 42–45 minutes (do not overbake; bars should be slightly gooey). Transfer to a wire rack and cool completely. Cut into bars or squares. Cover and store in refrigerator.

Makes 24 large or 36 small bars.

Peanut Butter–Chocolate Gooey Chess Squares

Lemon-Blueberry Gooey Chess Squares

A box of yellow cake mix is suddenly elegant thanks to a little imagination and a handful of summer berries. You can substitute fresh or frozen (thawed) blackberries or raspberries in this recipe for an equally delicious, decadent result. An equal amount of diced fresh apricots or peaches is also excellent here at the height of the harvest.

1	cup (2 sticks) butter, divided
1	18.25-ounce package yellow cake mix
4	large eggs
1	8-ounce package cream cheese, softened
6	tablespoons fresh lemon juice
2	tablespoons grated lemon zest
1	16-ounce box powdered sugar
2	cups fresh blueberries or 2 cups frozen (thawed) blueberries, drained and patted dry

Preheat oven to 350° (or 325° for dark-coated metal pan). Position oven rack in middle of oven. Spray the bottom only of a 13 x 9-inch metal baking pan with nonstick cooking spray (or foil-line pan; see page 11).

Melt ½ cup (1 stick) of the butter in a small saucepan set over low heat. In a large bowl beat the cake mix, melted butter, and 1 egg with an electric mixer set on medium speed until well blended (mixture will come together as a thick dough). Pat the dough evenly into the prepared pan. Set aside momentarily.

Melt the remaining stick of butter in a small saucepan set over low heat. In a large bowl beat the softened cream cheese, lemon juice, and lemon zest with an electric mixer set on medium speed until blended and smooth, scraping down sides of bowl occasionally. Add the melted butter and remaining 3 eggs; blend until smooth. Add the powdered sugar; blend until smooth. Stir in the blueberries.

Spread lemon-blueberry mixture over prepared crust. Bake 42–45 minutes (do not overbake; bars should be slightly gooey). Transfer to a wire rack and cool completely. Cut into bars or squares. Cover and store in refrigerator.

Variation:

Fresh Cranberry Orange Chess Squares: Prepare as directed above but substitute orange juice for the lemon juice, orange zest for the lemon zest, and fresh or frozen (thawed) cranberries for the blueberries.

Makes 24 large or 36 small bars.

Triple-Chocolate Gooey Chess Squares

A chocolate lover's dream come true, these decadent chess squares are memorable after one bite. Their deep, rich flavor stems from chocolate times three: chocolate cake mix, cocoa powder in the filling, and miniature chocolate chips throughout.

1	cup (2 sticks) butter, divided
1	18.25-ounce package chocolate cake mix
3	large eggs
1	8-ounce package cream cheese, softened
5	tablespoons unsweetened cocoa powder
2	teaspoons vanilla extract
1	16-ounce box powdered sugar
¾	cup miniature semisweet chocolate chips

Preheat oven to 350° (or 325° for dark-coated metal pan). Position oven rack in middle of oven. Spray the bottom only of a 13 x 9-inch metal baking pan with nonstick cooking spray (or foil-line pan; see page 11).

Melt ½ cup (1 stick) of the butter in a small saucepan set over low heat. In a large bowl beat the cake mix, melted butter, and 1 egg with an electric mixer set on medium speed until well blended. Pat the dough evenly into the prepared pan. Set aside momentarily.

Melt the remaining stick of butter in a small saucepan set over low heat. In a large bowl beat the softened cream cheese, cocoa powder, and vanilla extract with an electric mixer set on medium speed until blended and smooth, scraping down sides of bowl occasionally. Add the melted butter and remaining 2 eggs; blend until smooth. Add the powdered sugar; blend until smooth. Stir in chocolate chips.

Spread cream cheese mixture over prepared crust. Bake 42–45 minutes (do not overbake; bars should be slightly gooey). Transfer to a wire rack and cool completely. Cut into bars or squares. Cover and store in refrigerator.

Makes 24 large or 36 small bars.

Banana Monkey Bars

What are you waiting for? Anytime is a good time to get together with friends and family—and bring along a great recipe you can share and you'll soon be known for. Like these quick and delicious banana bars that are made with ingredients likely in your pantry already.

1   18.25-ounce package yellow cake mix
⅓   cup vegetable oil
1   large egg
1   cup chopped nuts (e.g., peanuts, walnuts, or pecans)
1   14-ounce can sweetened condensed milk
1   cup mashed banana (about 2 medium bananas)
1   cup butterscotch baking chips (or milk chocolate chips)
1⅓ cups sweetened flaked coconut

Preheat oven to 350° (or 325° for dark-coated metal pan). Position oven rack in middle of oven. Spray the bottom only of a 13 x 9-inch metal baking pan with nonstick cooking spray (or foil-line pan; see page 11).

In a large bowl beat cake mix, oil, and egg with electric mixer set on medium speed until well blended and crumbly. Stir in the nuts. Set aside 1 cup of the crumb mixture. Firmly press remaining crumb mixture on bottom of prepared pan.

In small bowl combine condensed milk and mashed banana; pour evenly over crust. Top with butterscotch chips and coconut; press down firmly. Sprinkle with reserved crumb mixture.

Bake 25–28 minutes or until lightly browned. Transfer to wire rack and cool completely. Cut into bars.

Makes 24 large or 36 small bars.

Tennessee Jam Cake Streusel Bars

Tennessee Jam Cake is a classic Southern dessert made with layers of spice cake, blackberry jam (sometimes stirred into the batter, sometimes spread between the layers of cake) and finished with penuche (caramel fudge) frosting. Heaven. Here the same flavor is captured in an impressive, but still easy, streusel bar.

1	18.25-ounce package spice cake mix
1	cup (2 sticks) butter, melted
1	teaspoon pumpkin pie spice (or ground cinnamon)
2	cups quick-cooking oats
1	12-ounce jar blackberry jam or preserves
1	cup butterscotch baking chips
½	cup chopped pecans (or walnuts)

Preheat oven to 350° (or 325° for dark-coated metal pan). Position oven rack in middle of oven. Spray the bottom only of a 13 x 9-inch metal baking pan with nonstick cooking spray (or foil-line pan; see page 11).

In a large bowl place the cake mix, melted butter, and pumpkin pie spice. Blend with an electric mixer set on medium speed 1–2 minutes, until blended and smooth. Mix in the oats with a wooden spoon until combined. Press half of the mixture evenly into prepared pan.

Spoon and spread blackberry jam over prepared crust. Add butterscotch chips and nuts to remaining crumb mixture; sprinkle over bars and press down gently.

Bake 30–34 minutes or until topping is set and firm to the touch. Transfer to wire rack and cool completely. Cut into bars.

Makes 24 large or 36 small bars.

Viennese Almond Teacakes

The Berkeley coffeehouse where I worked for many years served a moist, dense almond cake that I have been unable to forget. This very easy version comes very close to replicating the original. An added bonus is that they keep and travel extremely well. The almond filling (not to be confused with almond paste or marzipan) can be found in the baking section of most supermarkets alongside the fruit pie fillings.

1	18.25-ounce package yellow cake mix
1	12.5-ounce can almond filling
⅓	cup butter, melted
2	large eggs
⅓	cup powdered sugar

Preheat oven to 350° (or 325° for dark-coated metal pan). Position oven rack in middle of oven. Spray the bottom only of a 13 x 9-inch metal baking pan with nonstick cooking spray (or foil-line pan; see page 11).

In a large bowl mix half of the cake mix, the almond filling, melted butter, and eggs with an electric mixer set on medium-high speed 1–2 minutes, until well blended and smooth. Stir in remaining cake mix with a wooden spoon until all dry ingredients are moistened and well blended (mixture will be thick). Press dough into prepared pan.

Bake 22–25 minutes or until just set at edges. Transfer to wire rack and cool completely. Cut into bars. Sift with powdered sugar.

Variation:

Chocolate Chocolate-Chip Almond Teacakes: Prepare as directed above but substitute chocolate cake mix for yellow cake mix and add 1 cup miniature semisweet chocolate chips to the batter.

Makes 24 large or 36 small bars.

Double Chocolate Brownies

Who knew that five ingredients and five minutes of prep time could lead to such chocolate pleasure? Be sure to add another 15 seconds to pour a glass of cold milk. Superb plain, they can be gussied up in numerous ways, as the variations below indicate.

1	18.25-ounce package chocolate cake mix
⅓	cup butter, melted
2	large eggs
2	teaspoons vanilla extract
1	cup semisweet chocolate chips

Preheat oven to 350° (or 325° for dark-coated metal pan). Position oven rack in middle of oven. Spray the bottom only of a 13 x 9-inch metal baking pan with nonstick cooking spray (or foil-line pan; see page 11).

In a large bowl mix half of the cake mix along with the melted butter, eggs, and vanilla extract with an electric mixer set on medium-high speed 1–2 minutes, until well blended and smooth. Stir in remaining cake mix and chocolate chips with a wooden spoon until all dry ingredients are moistened and well blended (mixture will be thick). Press dough into prepared pan.

Bake 22–25 minutes or until just set at edges. Transfer to wire rack and cool completely. Cut into bars.

Variations:

Espresso Ganache Brownies: Prepare as directed above but eliminate semisweet chocolate chips and add 1 tablespoon instant espresso or coffee powder to batter. After baking, spread completely cooled brownies with Chocolate Ganache (see page 207).

Walnut Fudge Brownies: Prepare as directed above but eliminate semisweet chocolate chips and add 1 cup chopped walnuts to batter. After baking, spread completely cooled brownies with Chocolate Fudge Frosting (see page 208).

White Chocolate Candy Cane Brownies: Prepare as directed above but eliminate semisweet chocolate chips. Transfer baked brownies to wire rack and immediately sprinkle with 2 cups white chocolate chips; let stand 5 minutes until softened but not melted. Using a table knife, spread the white chocolate evenly over brownies; immediately sprinkle with ⅔ cup crushed peppermint candy canes or striped peppermint candies.

Makes 24 large or 36 small bars.

S'mores Brownies

Here is a delicious brownie-based interpretation of the classic campfire classic.

1¾ cups graham cracker crumbs
2   tablespoons sugar
1   cup (2 sticks) butter, melted, divided
1   18.25-ounce package chocolate fudge cake mix
⅔   cup (1 5-ounce can) evaporated milk
1   cup miniature semisweet chocolate chips
3½ cups miniature marshmallows

Preheat oven to 350° (or 325° for dark-coated metal pan). Position oven rack in middle of oven. Foil-line a 13 x 9-inch baking pan (see page 11).

In a medium bowl combine the graham cracker crumbs, sugar, and half (1 stick) of the melted butter until well blended. Press crumb mixture evenly into bottom of foil-lined pan. Bake 5 minutes.

Meanwhile, in a large bowl mix the cake mix, remaining ½ cup melted butter, evaporated milk, and miniature chocolate chips with an electric mixer set on medium speed 1–2 minutes, until all dry ingredients are moistened and well blended (batter will be thick). Carefully spread batter over graham cracker crust.

Bake 22–25 minutes or until just set at edges. Remove from oven and turn oven to broil setting. Position oven rack 8–10 inches from heat source. Evenly sprinkle brownies with marshmallows. Broil 1–3 minutes longer, until marshmallows are puffed and browned (watch carefully to avoid scorching; marshmallows should still hold their shape).

Transfer to wire rack and cool completely. Cut into bars with knife sprayed with nonstick cooking spray.

Makes 24 large or 36 small bars.

Chocolate Caramel Brownies

A voluptuous combination of caramel and chocolate comprise these mouthwatering brownies. Share them—it's certain they will create countless new friendships and fond memories.

1   **18.25-ounce package chocolate fudge cake mix**
1   **cup chopped pecans (or walnuts)**
1   **cup canned evaporated milk, divided**
½   **cup (1 stick) butter, melted**
35   **caramels, unwrapped**
2   **cups semisweet chocolate chips**

Preheat oven to 350° (or 325° for dark-coated metal pan). Position oven rack in middle of oven. Spray the bottom only of a 13 x 9-inch metal baking pan with nonstick cooking spray (or foil-line pan; see page 11).

In large bowl place half the cake mix along with the nuts, ⅔ cup evaporated milk, and melted butter. Blend with electric mixer on medium speed 1–2 minutes, until all dry ingredients are moistened and well blended (batter will be thick). Spread half of the batter into prepared pan.

Bake 10 minutes.

Meanwhile, in small saucepan over low heat melt caramels and remaining ⅓ cup evaporated milk, stirring constantly, until caramels are melted. Sprinkle chocolate chips over partially baked brownie; drizzle with caramel mixture. Drop remaining batter by heaping spoonfuls over caramel mixture.

Bake 24–27 minutes or until center is set and firm to the touch. Transfer to wire rack and cool completely. Cut into bars.

Variations:

Snickery-good Brownies: Prepare as directed above but eliminate the caramel filling (the 35 caramels and the remaining ⅓ cup evaporated milk) and chocolate chips. Instead, sprinkle the partially baked crust with 6 coarsely chopped caramel nougat chocolate bars (e.g., Snickers®); drop remaining batter by heaping spoonfuls over chocolate bars. Continue baking as directed above.

Peanut-Butterscotch Layered Brownies: Prepare as directed above but eliminate the caramel filling (the 35 caramels and the remaining ⅓ cup evaporated milk) and chocolate chips. Instead, melt 1⅓ cups butterscotch baking chips with ½ cup creamy peanut butter in a saucepan set over low heat. Spoon and spread mixture over the partially baked crust; drop remaining batter by heaping spoonfuls over butterscotch layer. Continue baking as directed above.

Makes 24 large or 36 small bars.

Chocolate Caramel Brownies

Carrot Cake Bars

I'd like to convince myself that eating one of these moist, cream cheese–topped bars is not an exercise in indulgence but rather good health. After all, carrots have been revered for their nutritional benefits for more than 2000 years. You might just have to eat two to be on the safe side.

1	18.25-ounce package carrot cake or spice cake mix
⅔	cup vegetable oil
3	large eggs
1	cup shredded, peeled carrots
1	cup raisins (or dried cranberries)
1	cup chopped pecans, optional
1	recipe Cream Cheese Frosting (see page 212)

Preheat oven to 350° (or 325° for dark-coated metal pan). Position oven rack in middle of oven. Spray the bottom only of a 13 x 9-inch metal baking pan with nonstick cooking spray (or foil-line pan; see page 11).

In a large bowl mix the cake mix, oil, and eggs with an electric mixer on low speed for 30 seconds. Scrape down the sides of the bowl. Increase the mixer speed to medium and beat 1–2 minutes more, or until batter is smooth and very thick. Stir in the carrots, raisins, and pecans with a wooden spoon.

Spread the batter into the prepared pan; pressing out to cover the bottom (dough will spread as it bakes).

Bake 22–25 minutes or until just set at center (do not overbake). Transfer to a wire rack and cool completely. Prepare Cream Cheese Frosting; spread over cooled bars. Cut into bars or squares.

Makes 24 large or 36 small bars.

Baklava Bars

The flavor of baklava—a butter-rich, many-layered Greek pastry, rich with spices, nuts, and lemon—is simplified here in an easy-to-prepare bar recipe.

1	18.25-ounce package yellow cake mix
¾	cup (1½ sticks) butter, melted, divided
4	large eggs
1	cup packed light brown sugar
1	cup honey
2	teaspoons grated lemon zest
2	teaspoons vanilla extract
½	teaspoon ground cinnamon
1½	cups chopped walnuts

Preheat oven to 350° (or 325° for dark-coated metal pan). Position oven rack in middle of oven. Spray an 13 x 9-inch metal baking pan with nonstick cooking spray (or foil-line pan; see page 11).

Place the cake mix and ½ cup melted butter in a large bowl. Blend with an electric mixer set on medium speed until blended and crumbly. Press mixture into the prepared pan.

Bake 15 minutes.

While crust bakes, in a large mixing bowl beat the eggs with a fork. Whisk in the brown sugar, honey, remaining ¼ cup melted butter, lemon zest, vanilla extract, and cinnamon; stir in the walnuts. Spread mixture evenly over warm base layer.

Bake an additional 40–45 minutes or until filling is set. Transfer to a wire rack and cool completely. Cut into bars.

Makes 24 large or 36 small bars.

Pecan Pie Bars

These decadent dessert bars are dedicated to all my fellow cookie aficionados who cannot resist the pecan pie bars in the coffeehouse pastry case. Great with a cup of coffee at any time of the year, they can also replace traditional pecan pie when you need to serve a crowd.

1   18.25-ounce package yellow cake mix
⅓   cup butter, softened
4   large eggs
½   cup firmly packed dark brown sugar
1½   cups dark corn syrup
1½   teaspoons vanilla extract
1¼   cups chopped pecans, divided

Preheat oven to 350° (or 325° for dark-coated metal pan). Position oven rack in middle of oven. Spray the bottom only of a 13x9-inch metal baking pan with nonstick cooking spray (or foil-line pan; see page 11).

Set aside ⅔ cup of the dry cake mix. In a large bowl mix remaining cake mix, softened butter, and 1 of the eggs with an electric mixer set on medium speed until blended and crumbly. Press mixture in bottom of prepared pan.

Bake 15 minutes.

Meanwhile, in large bowl mix reserved ⅔ cup cake mix, brown sugar, corn syrup, vanilla extract, and remaining 3 eggs with electric mixer set on low speed for 1 minute.

Increase speed to medium; blend 1 minute. Stir in ¾ cup chopped pecans. Pour mixture over hot crust; sprinkle with remaining pecans.

Bake an additional 30–35 minutes or until filling is set. Transfer to wire rack and cool completely. Cut into bars.

Variation:

Chocolate-Chip Pecan Pie Bars: Prepare as directed above but use chocolate cake mix and add 1 cup miniature semisweet chocolate chips to the filling.

Makes 24 large or 36 small bars

Fresh Blackberry-Lemon Crumb Bars

Think summer, then think refreshing and sweet. Lemons come to mind?
Let this easy lemon bar cookie, bursting with blackberries, celebrate the picnics,
parties, and barbecues to come. Raspberries or blueberries may be used
in place of the blackberries for delicious variations.

1	18.25-ounce package yellow cake mix
½	cup (1 stick) butter, softened
1	large egg
1	tablespoon grated lemon zest
1	14-ounce can sweetened condensed milk
½	cup fresh-squeezed lemon juice
2	cups fresh or frozen (thawed) blackberries

Preheat oven to 350° (or 325° for dark-coated metal pan). Position oven rack in middle of oven. Spray the bottom only of a 13 x 9-inch metal baking pan with nonstick cooking spray (or foil-line pan; see page 11).

In large bowl place the cake mix, softened butter, and egg. Blend with an electric mixer set on low speed until all dry ingredients are moistened and mixture is well blended and crumbly. Press half of mixture evenly into bottom of prepared pan.

Bake 15 minutes.

Meanwhile, in a medium bowl whisk together the lemon zest and condensed milk with the lemon juice. Stir until well-blended.

Arrange blackberries evenly over surface of partially baked crust. Pour lemon mixture over blackberries as evenly as possible; sprinkle with reserved crumb mixture.

Bake 20–24 minutes or until topping is golden brown. Transfer to wire rack and cool completely. Cut into bars. Store in the refrigerator.

Makes 24 large or 36 small bars.

Tiramisu Bars

Tiramisu was a nineties hit, seemingly appearing on most every dessert menu around. But while the fad has faded, the popularity of the ambrosial Italian concoction of cream and cake has not. Here it finds new life as inspiration for an easily assembled bar cookie. Buon appetito!

2	teaspoons vanilla extract, divided
1	tablespoon instant espresso (or coffee powder)
1	18.25-ounce package white cake mix, divided
¼	cup (½ stick) butter, melted
4	large eggs
1½	cups chocolate-covered toffee baking bits, divided
2	cups ricotta cheese
1	14-ounce can sweetened condensed milk
2½	tablespoons dark rum

Preheat oven to 350° (or 325° for dark-coated metal pan). Position oven rack in middle of oven. Spray the bottom only of a 13x9-inch metal baking pan with nonstick cooking spray (or foil-line pan; see page 11).

In a large mixing bowl mix 1 teaspoon vanilla extract with espresso powder until dissolved. Measure out ½ cup of the cake mix; set aside. Add the remaining cake mix, melted butter, 1 egg, and ½ cup toffee bits into bowl with espresso mixture. Blend with electric mixer set on low speed 2 minutes; scrape down bowl. Beat 30 seconds longer. Press mixture into prepared pan. Set aside momentarily.

In the same large bowl blend the ricotta cheese and condensed milk with electric mixer set on low speed 1 minute. Add reserved ½ cup cake mix, remaining 1 teaspoon vanilla extract, remaining 3 eggs, and rum and blend with electric mixer set on medium speed 1 minute, until well blended. Pour and spread evenly over prepared crust. Sprinkle evenly with remaining 1 cup toffee bits.

Bake 48–52 minutes or until center is just barely set when pan is jiggled (do not overbake). Transfer to wire rack and cool completely. Refrigerate at least 4 hours or overnight. Cut into bars.

Makes 36 medium bars or 48 small squares.

Chocolate Cheesecake Bars

Sure to make chocoholic hearts beat faster, these enticing confections combine a velvet cheesecake and chocolate filling with even more chocolate in the base. Irresistible.

1	18.25-ounce package chocolate cake mix
3	large eggs
⅓	cup butter, melted
2	8-ounce packages cream cheese
1	cup sour cream
1½	cups semisweet chocolate chips

Preheat oven to 350° (or 325° for dark-coated metal pan). Position oven rack in middle of oven. Spray the bottom only of a 13 x 9-inch metal baking pan with nonstick cooking spray (or foil-line pan; see page 11).

Reserve 1 cup of cake mix; set aside. In a medium bowl place the remaining cake mix, 1 of the eggs, and melted butter. Blend with an electric mixer set on medium speed until all dry ingredients are moistened. Press mixture into prepared pan.

Bake 10 minutes.

Meanwhile, in a medium bowl beat the reserved cake mix, remaining 2 eggs, cream cheese, and sour cream with an electric mixer set on medium speed until blended and smooth; fold in chocolate chips. Spread cream cheese mixture over crust.

Bake 30–35 minutes or until just barely set. Transfer to wire rack and cool completely. Refrigerate at least 2 hours before serving. Cut into bars.

Variations:

Chocolate-Raspberry Cheesecake Bars: Prepare as directed above but dollop ⅔ cup seedless raspberry preserves in teaspoons over surface of cheesecake batter before baking; swirl batter and preserves with tip of a kitchen knife.

White Chocolate–Lemon Cheesecake Bars: Prepare as directed above but substitute lemon cake mix for the chocolate cake mix. Reduce sour cream to ¾ cup and add ¼ cup fresh lemon juice to cream cheese batter. Substitute white chocolate chips for the semisweet chocolate chips.

White Chocolate–Latte Cheesecake Bars: Prepare as directed above but substitute vanilla cake mix for the chocolate cake mix. Add 2½ teaspoons instant espresso or coffee powder dissolved in 2 teaspoons vanilla extract into the cream cheese batter and substitute white chocolate chips for the semisweet chocolate chips.

Irish Cream–Milk Chocolate Cheesecake Bars: Prepare as directed above but substitute vanilla cake mix for the chocolate cake mix, ½ cup Irish cream liqueur for ½ cup of the sour cream, and milk chocolate chips for the semisweet chocolate chips.

Makes 24 large or 36 small bars.

Mandarin Orange Cheesecake Bars

Mandarin oranges and cheesecake? Oh yes. This is the kind of recipe home bakers dream about: so simple, so beautiful, and so delicious that everyone will want to linger to have a second or third helping. The fresh flavors of this bar make it a great choice for spring and summer get-togethers.

1	18.25-ounce package yellow cake mix
3	large eggs
⅓	cup butter, melted
2	8-ounce packages of cream cheese
⅔	cup sour cream
⅓	cup orange marmalade
1	11-ounce can mandarin oranges, drained

Preheat oven to 350° (or 325° for dark-coated metal pan). Position oven rack in middle of oven. Spray the bottom only of a 13 x 9-inch metal baking pan with non-stick cooking spray (or foil-line pan; see page 11).

Reserve 1 cup of cake mix; set aside. In a medium bowl place the remaining cake mix, 1 of the eggs, and melted butter. Blend with an electric mixer set on medium speed until all dry ingredients are moistened. Press mixture into prepared pan.

Bake 10 minutes.

Meanwhile, in a medium bowl beat the reserved cake mix, remaining 2 eggs, cream cheese, sour cream, and marmalade with an electric mixer set on medium speed until blended and smooth; fold in mandarin oranges. Spread cream cheese mixture over crust.

Bake 30–35 minutes or until just barely set. Transfer to wire rack and cool completely. Refrigerate at least 2 hours before serving. Cut into bars.

Variation:

Ginger-Lime Cheesecake Bars: Prepare as directed above but add 2 teaspoons ground ginger to the cake mix-egg-butter mixture, use lime juice in place of the marmalade, and eliminate the mandarin oranges.

Makes 24 large or 36 small bars.

German Chocolate Bars

Delight chocolate aficionados with this gooey cookie bar that showcases chocolate in all its decadent glory.

1	18.25-ounce package German chocolate cake mix
⅓	cup butter, softened
2	large eggs
1	14-ounce can sweetened condensed milk
1	teaspoon vanilla extract
1⅓	cups flaked sweetened coconut, divided
1	cup chopped pecans
1½	cups milk chocolate chips, divided

Preheat oven to 350° (or 325° for dark-coated metal pan). Position oven rack in middle of oven. Spray the bottom only of a 13 x 9-inch metal baking pan with nonstick cooking spray (or foil-line pan; see page 11).

In a large bowl place the cake mix, softened butter, and 1 of the eggs. Blend 1–2 minutes with an electric mixer set on low speed until well blended. Press mixture in bottom of prepared pan.

In a medium bowl whisk the condensed milk, remaining egg, and vanilla extract until well blended. Stir in 1 cup coconut, pecans, and ¾ cup milk chocolate chips. Spread mixture evenly over crust. Sprinkle with remaining coconut and chocolate chips; lightly press into condensed milk layer.

Bake 30–32 minutes or until center is almost set. Center will firm when cool. Transfer to wire rack and cool completely. Cut into bars.

Makes 24 large or 36 small bars.

Lemon Macaroon Bars

*A memorable dessert is something to be proud of, whether hosting
a fancy dinner party or just throwing something together for the family
some weeknight or weekend. No matter what the occasion,
this is an easy option that will make any home baker beam
and blush from all of the kudos.*

1	18.25-ounce package lemon cake mix
⅓	cup butter, softened
2	large eggs
1	14-ounce can sweetened condensed milk
2	tablespoons lemon juice
1	tablespoon grated lemon zest
2⅔	cups (1 7-ounce bag) flaked sweetened coconut, divided

Preheat oven to 350° (or 325° for dark-coated metal pan). Position oven rack in middle of oven. Spray the bottom only of a 13 x 9-inch metal baking pan with nonstick cooking spray (or foil-line pan; see page 11).

In a large bowl place the cake mix, softened butter and 1 of the eggs. Blend 1–2 minutes with an electric mixer set on low speed until well blended. Press mixture in bottom of prepared pan.

In a medium bowl whisk the condensed milk, remaining egg, lemon juice and lemon zest until well blended. Stir in 1⅓ cups coconut; spread mixture evenly over base. Sprinkle with remaining coconut; lightly press into condensed milk layer.

Bake 28–30 minutes or until center is almost set. Center will firm when cool. Transfer to wire rack and cool completely. Cut into bars.

Variation:

Vanilla Macaroon Bars: Prepare as directed above but use vanilla cake mix in place of lemon cake mix and use 2 teaspoons vanilla extract in place of the lemon juice and lemon zest.

Makes 24 large or 36 small bars.

Premier Cranberry Cream Cheese Bars

Dazzle those dear to you during the winter holidays, or year-round, with these easy-to-make, beautiful-to-behold bars.

1	18.25-ounce package spice cake mix
1	cup (2 sticks) butter, melted
2¼	cups quick-cooking oats
1	cup white chocolate chips
1	8-ounce package cream cheese, softened
1	14-ounce can sweetened condensed milk
¼	cup fresh lemon juice
1	teaspoon vanilla extract
2	tablespoons cornstarch
1	16-ounce can whole cranberry sauce

Preheat oven to 350° (or 325° for dark-coated metal pan). Position oven rack in middle of oven. Spray the bottom only of a 13x9-inch metal baking pan with nonstick cooking spray (or foil-line pan; see page 11).

In a large bowl place the cake mix and melted butter. Blend 1–2 minutes with an electric mixer set on low speed until well blended. Stir in oats with a wooden spoon. Press half of mixture evenly into prepared pan. Add white chocolate chips to remaining oat mixture; set aside.

In a large mixing bowl beat the softened cream cheese, condensed milk, lemon juice, and vanilla extract with electric mixer set on medium speed until blended and smooth. Spoon and spread cream cheese mixture over prepared crust.

In a small bowl stir together the cornstarch and cranberry sauce until well blended; spoon over cream cheese mixture. Top with reserved crumb mixture and press down gently.

Bake 35–38 minutes or until topping is set and firm to the touch. Transfer to wire rack and cool completely.

Makes 24 large or 36 small bars.

Premier Cranberry Cream Cheese Bars

Peanut Brittle Bars

This satisfying, candy-like finale features all the flavors of homemade peanut brittle. With a few simple steps, you'll impress any dessert lover.

1   18.25-ounce package yellow cake mix
1⅓ cups creamy peanut butter, divided
1   large egg
½   cup vegetable oil
1   14-ounce can sweetened condensed milk
2   teaspoons vanilla extract
1   10-ounce bag toffee baking bits
2   cups lightly salted roasted peanuts

Preheat oven to 350° (or 325° for dark-coated metal pan). Position oven rack in middle of oven. Spray the bottom only of a 13x9-inch metal baking pan with nonstick cooking spray (or foil-line pan; see page 11).

In a large bowl place the cake mix, 1 cup peanut butter, egg, and oil. Blend 1–2 minutes with an electric mixer set on low speed, until well blended (mixture will be stiff and crumbly). Press two-thirds of mixture into prepared pan.

Bake 10 minutes.

Meanwhile, in a medium bowl whisk the condensed milk, remaining ⅓ cup peanut butter, and vanilla extract until blended and smooth. Stir in half of the toffee bits; pour over crust. Sprinkle with peanuts, remaining crumb mixture, and remaining toffee bits.

Bake 20–25 minutes or until golden brown and topping is firm to the touch.

Transfer to wire rack and cool completely. Cut into bars.

Makes 24 large or 36 small bars.

Spiced Apple Butter Bars with Apple Butter–Cream Cheese Frosting

After-school snacks have never been better than with this home-style bar. The Apple Butter–Cream Cheese Frosting adds a luxurious smoothness to these moist bars, which happen to keep extremely well.

1	18.25-ounce package spice cake mix
1	large egg
¼	cup vegetable oil
1	cup apple butter, divided
1	cup chopped walnuts
1	8-ounce package cream cheese, softened
¼	teaspoon ground cinnamon
3½	cups powdered sugar

Preheat oven to 350° (or 325° for dark-coated metal pan). Position oven rack in middle of oven. Spray the bottom only of a 13 x 9-inch metal baking pan with nonstick cooking spray (or foil-line pan; see page 11).

In a large bowl place the cake mix, egg, oil, and ½ cup of the apple butter. Blend 1–2 minutes with an electric mixer set on low speed until well blended. Spread evenly into the prepared pan. Sprinkle with walnuts.

Bake 30–35 minutes until lightly browned and firm to the touch. Transfer to wire rack and cool completely.

In a medium bowl beat softened cream cheese, remaining ½ cup apple butter, and cinnamon with mixer set on medium speed. Beat in powdered sugar until frosting is fluffy. Spread frosting over cooled bars. Cut into bars.

Makes 24 large or 36 small bars.

Lemon Buttermilk Bars

I'm a firm believer in making the most of the summer months. The living, as an old song suggests, should be easy, the food, light. With that said, these treats are indispensable. The buttermilk brightens the lemon for a very citrusy, very summery bar (plain yogurt can be used in place of the buttermilk for equally good results). The only other items needed are a glass of iced tea, a good book, and a few hours of nothing else to do.

1	18.25-ounce package lemon cake mix
4	large eggs
¾	cup (1½ sticks) butter, melted, divided
¾	cup buttermilk
¼	cup fresh lemon juice
⅓	cup sugar
1	tablespoon grated lemon zest
1–2	tablespoons powdered sugar

Preheat oven to 350° (or 325° for dark-coated metal pan). Position oven rack in middle of oven. Spray the bottom only of a 13x9-inch metal baking pan with nonstick cooking spray (or foil-line pan; see page 11).

Reserve 1 cup of the cake mix; set aside. In a large bowl place remaining cake mix, 1 of the eggs, and ¼ cup melted butter. Blend 1–2 minutes with an electric mixer set on low speed until well blended. Press mixture into bottom of prepared pan.

In a medium bowl mix remaining 3 eggs, buttermilk, lemon juice, remaining ½ cup melted butter, sugar, and lemon zest with electric mixer set on low speed until well blended. Add reserved cake mix, beating 2 minutes on medium speed until mixture is smooth; pour over prepared crust.

Bake 35–38 minutes, until just set and light golden on top. Transfer to wire rack and cool completely. Cut into bars and sift with powdered sugar.

Makes 24 large or 36 small bars.

Deep Dark Chocolate Sour Cream Bars

Surrender to the sublime. Smooth and deeply chocolate, chocoholics will be hard-pressed to find a more opulent option.

1	18.25-ounce package chocolate fudge cake mix
4	large eggs
¾	cup (1½ sticks) butter, melted, divided
1	cup sour cream (not reduced fat)
⅓	cup light brown sugar, packed
2	cups semisweet chocolate chips
1–2	tablespoons unsweetened cocoa powder

Preheat oven to 350° (or 325° for dark-coated metal pan). Position oven rack in middle of oven. Spray the bottom only of a 13 x 9-inch metal baking pan with nonstick cooking spray (or foil-line pan; see page 11).

Reserve 1 cup of the cake mix; set aside. In a large bowl place remaining cake mix, 1 of the eggs, and ¼ cup melted butter. Blend 1–2 minutes with an electric mixer set on low speed until well blended. Press mixture into prepared pan.

In medium bowl mix remaining 3 eggs, sour cream, brown sugar, and remaining ½ cup melted butter with electric mixer set on low speed until well blended. Add reserved cake mix, beating 2 minutes on medium speed until mixture is smooth; stir in chocolate chips. Pour over prepared crust.

Bake for 35–38 minutes, until just set and light golden on top. Transfer to wire rack and cool completely. Cut into bars and sift with cocoa powder.

Makes 24 large or 36 small bars.

Peanut Butter Fudge Bars

*Just like politics, dessert preferences are local. Maybe you're
partial to Georgia peach cobbler. Or perhaps California coconut-lime
ice cream or a New England cranberry betty is your style.
But one thing's for certain: these over-the-top peanut butter–
chocolate fudge bars bridge all boundaries.*

1	18.25-ounce package yellow cake mix
1	cup creamy peanut butter
2	large eggs
½	cup vegetable oil
2	cups semisweet chocolate chips
1	14-ounce can sweetened condensed milk
2	tablespoons butter
2	teaspoons vanilla extract

Preheat oven to 350° (or 325° for dark-coated metal pan). Position oven rack in middle of oven. Spray the bottom only of a 13x9-inch metal baking pan with nonstick cooking spray (or foil-line pan; see page 11).

In a large bowl place the cake mix, peanut butter, eggs, and oil. Blend 1–2 minutes with an electric mixer set on low speed until well blended. Reserve 1½ cups of the mixture. Press remaining mixture into bottom of prepared pan; set pan and reserved mixture aside.

Meanwhile, in a heavy saucepan set over low heat, melt the chocolate chips with the condensed milk and butter, stirring until blended and smooth. Remove from heat and stir in vanilla extract; pour over crust. Sprinkle with remaining crumb mixture.

Bake 20–25 minutes or until golden brown and topping is firm to the touch.

Transfer to wire rack and cool completely. Cut into bars.

Variations:

Double Peanut Butter Fudge Bars: Prepare as directed above but substitute 2 cups peanut butter–flavored baking chips for the chocolate chips.

Double Chocolate Peanut Butter Fudge Bars: Prepare as directed above but use a chocolate cake mix instead of yellow cake mix.

Chocolate Hazelnut Fudge Bars: Prepare as directed above but use a chocolate cake mix instead of yellow cake mix and use chocolate-hazelnut spread in place of the peanut butter.

Makes 24 large or 36 small bars.

Pumpkin Pie Bars

This extra-easy take on everybody's Thanksgiving favorite brings
easy entertaining up to date.

1	18.25-ounce package yellow cake mix
¼	cup vegetable oil
4	large eggs
½	cup chopped pecans
1	14-ounce can sweetened condensed milk
1	16-ounce can pumpkin purée
2	teaspoons vanilla extract
1½	teaspoons pumpkin pie spice

Preheat oven to 350° (or 325° for dark-coated metal pan). Position oven rack in middle of oven. Spray an 13x9-inch metal baking pan with nonstick cooking spray (or foil-line pan; see page 11).

Reserve ½ cup cake mix. In a large bowl place remaining cake mix, oil, and 1 of the eggs. Blend 1–2 minutes with an electric mixer set on low speed until well blended and crumbly; stir in the pecans. Press mixture into bottom of prepared pan.

Place the condensed milk, pumpkin, vanilla extract, pumpkin pie spice, remaining 3 eggs and ½ cup reserved cake mix in the same large bowl (no need to clean). Blend 1–2 minutes with an electric mixer set on medium speed until well blended. Pour over crust.

Bake 40–45 minutes or until filling is just set. Transfer to a wire rack and cool completely. Cut into bars.

Makes 24 large or 36 small bars.

Deluxe Chocolate Caramel Candy Bars

These luscious treats are a cross between a cookie and a candy bar. In other words, to die for. For a birthday treat, serve them warm, topped with a scoop of ice cream, sliced bananas, and fudge sauce for a brownie banana split. Don't forget the whipped cream, cherries, and nuts!

1   18.25-ounce package butter pecan cake mix
1   stick (½ cup) butter, melted
1   14-ounce can sweetened condensed milk
2   teaspoons vanilla extract
1½ cups coarsely chopped pecans
1½ cups sweetened flaked coconut
20 caramels, unwrapped
2   tablespoons milk
1   cup semisweet chocolate chips

Preheat oven to 350° (or 325° for dark-coated metal pan). Position oven rack in middle of oven. Spray an 13 x 9-inch metal baking pan with nonstick cooking spray (or foil-line pan; see page 11).

Place the cake mix and melted butter in a large bowl. Blend 1–2 minutes with an electric mixer set on low speed until well blended and crumbly. Press mixture into bottom of prepared pan.

Bake 10 minutes.

While crust bakes, in a large mixing bowl whisk together the condensed milk and vanilla extract. Sprinkle pecans and coconut over baked crust; pour condensed milk mixture over pecans and coconut.

Bake an additional 25–28 minutes or until filling is set and golden brown. Transfer to a wire rack and cool 10 minutes.

Meanwhile, in a small saucepan set over low heat melt the caramels with the milk, stirring until smooth; drizzle over partially cooled bars and sprinkle with chocolate chips. Cool completely. Cut into bars.

Makes 24 large or 36 small bars.

Deluxe Chocolate Caramel Candy Bars

Key Lime Bars

*Whether the weather is already warm or just heating up,
these chilled, tart, creamy bars have immense appeal. And even
though they are excellent served cold on a sultry day,
they are not exclusively hot-weather fare. It would be a shame to
limit such pleasures to only one season of the year!*

1   18.25-ounce package vanilla cake mix
1   stick (½ cup) butter, melted
1   large egg yolk
4   large eggs
1   14-ounce can sweetened condensed milk
⅔   cup lime juice
1   tablespoon grated lime zest

Preheat oven to 350° (or 325° for dark-coated metal pan). Position oven rack in middle of oven. Spray an 13 x 9-inch metal baking pan with nonstick cooking spray (or foil-line pan; see page 11).

Reserve 1 tablespoon cake mix. In a large bowl place the remaining cake mix, melted butter, and egg yolk. Blend 1–2 minutes with an electric mixer set on low speed until well blended and crumbly. Press mixture into bottom of prepared pan.

Bake 15 minutes.

While crust bakes, in a large mixing bowl whisk the eggs, condensed milk, lime juice, and reserved tablespoon of cake mix until blended and smooth; stir in lime zest. Carefully spread lime mixture over warm base layer.

Bake an additional 20–24 minutes or until topping is set and golden brown. Transfer to a wire rack and cool completely. Refrigerate until cold before serving, at least 2 hours. Cut into bars.

Variations:

Creamy Lemon Bars: Prepare as directed above but use lemon juice in place of the lime juice and lemon zest in place of the lime zest.

Orange Burst Bars: Prepare as directed above but use ½ cup orange juice plus 2½ tablespoons lemon juice in place of the lime juice and orange zest in place of the lime zest.

Key Lime Bars

Makes 24 large or 36 small bars.

Spicy Chocolate Aztec Bars

Kicked up with cayenne, coffee, cinnamon, and orange zest, these very rich, dark chocolate bars have gone south of the border.

1	18.25-ounce package devil's food cake mix
½	cup (1 stick) butter, melted
2	teaspoons grated orange peel
¾	teaspoon ground cinnamon
1	cup chopped nuts (almonds, pecans, or walnuts)
1½	cups semisweet chocolate chips
1	14-ounce can sweetened condensed milk
1	tablespoon instant espresso (or coffee powder)
⅛	teaspoon cayenne pepper

Preheat oven to 350° (or 325° for dark-coated metal pan). Position oven rack in middle of oven. Spray an 13 x 9-inch metal baking pan with nonstick cooking spray (or foil-line pan; see page 11).

In a large bowl place the cake mix, melted butter, orange peel, cinnamon, and nuts. Blend 1–2 minutes with an electric mixer set on low speed until well blended and crumbly. Press mixture into bottom of prepared pan.

Bake 15 minutes.

While crust bakes, in a medium saucepan set over low heat melt the chocolate chips with the condensed milk, stirring until smooth. Remove from heat and stir in espresso powder and cayenne until blended. Pour chocolate mixture over partially baked layer.

Bake an additional 20–22 minutes until just set. Transfer to a wire rack and cool completely. Cut into bars.

Makes 24 large or 36 small bars.

Butter Rum Bars with Coconut & Macadamia Nuts

*End your next summer BBQ on a sweet note
with these easy, island-inspired bars.*

1	18.25-ounce package yellow cake mix
½	cup (1 stick) butter, melted
1	14-ounce can sweetened condensed milk
2	large eggs
2	tablespoons dark rum (or 2 teaspoons rum-flavored extract)
1½	cups sweetened shredded coconut
1	cup chopped macadamia nuts
1	cup milk or white chocolate chips
1	tablespoon vegetable shortening

Preheat oven to 350° (or 325° for dark-coated metal pan). Position oven rack in middle of oven. Spray the bottom only of a 13 x 9-inch metal baking pan with nonstick cooking spray (or foil-line pan; see page 11).

In a large bowl place cake mix and melted butter. Blend 1–2 minutes with an electric mixer set on low speed until well blended and crumbly. Press mixture into bottom of prepared pan.

Bake 15 minutes.

While crust bakes, in a medium bowl whisk the condensed milk, eggs, and rum until blended; stir in coconut and macadamia nuts. Pour mixture over partially baked crust.

Bake 18–20 minutes longer or until golden at edges and just set at the center. Transfer to a wire rack.

In small saucepan set over low heat melt the chocolate chips with the shortening until melted and smooth. Drizzle over bars; cool completely.

Makes 24 large or 36 small bars.

Chocolate Revel Crumble Bars

They shouldn't be this easy. They shouldn't be this delicious.
But oh, how they are.

1	18.25-ounce package butter pecan cake mix
¼	cup packed dark brown sugar
1	cup (2 sticks) butter, melted
2	large eggs
2½	cups quick-cooking oats
2	cups semisweet chocolate chips
1	14-ounce can sweetened condensed milk
2	teaspoons vanilla extract
½	cup chopped pecans (or walnuts)

Preheat oven to 350° (or 325° for dark-coated metal pan). Position oven rack in middle of oven. Spray the bottom only of a 15 x 10 x 1-inch jelly roll pan with nonstick cooking spray (or foil-line pan; see page 11).

In a large bowl place the cake mix, brown sugar, melted butter and eggs. Blend 1–2 minutes with an electric mixer set on low speed until well blended and smooth. Stir in the oats by hand until combined. Press two-thirds of the oat mixture into bottom of prepared pan.

In a medium saucepan set over low heat melt the chocolate chips with the condensed milk, stirring until smooth. Remove from heat and stir in vanilla extract. Spread chocolate filling evenly over the oat crust. Add the nuts to remaining oat mixture; evenly distribute over the filling.

Bake 24–27 minutes or until topping is light brown (filling will still look slightly wet). Transfer to wire rack and cool. Cut into bars while still slightly warm.

Makes 36 large or 48 small bars.

Spiced & Iced Pumpkin Snack Bars

Mayonnaise is the secret ingredient in these tender, moist pumpkin bars. Be sure to use real mayonnaise (mostly eggs and oil) as opposed to salad dressing for optimal results.

1	18.25-ounce package spice cake mix
1	15-ounce can pumpkin purée
1	cup mayonnaise
3	large eggs
1½	teaspoons ground cinnamon, divided
1	cup dried cranberries (or raisins), optional
½	cup (1 stick) butter, softened
3½	cups powdered sugar
2	tablespoons milk
1	teaspoon vanilla extract

Preheat oven to 350° (or 325° for dark-coated metal pan). Position oven rack in middle of oven. Spray the bottom only of a 15 x 10 x 1-inch jelly roll pan with nonstick cooking spray (or foil-line pan; see page 11).

In a large bowl place the cake mix, pumpkin, mayonnaise, eggs, and 1 teaspoon cinnamon. Blend 2 minutes with an electric mixer set on medium speed until well blended and smooth. If desired, stir in dried cranberries. Pour and spread batter into prepared pan.

Bake 18–20 minutes or until toothpick inserted in center comes out clean. Transfer to wire rack and cool completely.

In a medium bowl beat the softened butter, powdered sugar, milk, vanilla extract and remaining ½ teaspoon cinnamon with electric mixer set on low speed 2 minutes. Beat on high speed until light and fluffy. Spread over cooled bars. Cut into bars. Store leftover bars in refrigerator.

Makes 36 large or 48 small bars.

Spiced & Iced Pumpkin Snack Bars

Apple-Cranberry Snack Bars

These sound like ideal autumn bars, and indeed they are. But don't wait until the leaves turn to give them a try—they are year-round winners.

1	18.25-ounce package spice cake mix
¾	cup mayonnaise
2	large eggs
1	cup chopped peeled tart apples (e.g., Granny Smith)
1	cup dried cranberries (or raisins)
½	cup (1 stick) butter, softened
3½	cups powdered sugar
2	tablespoons lemon juice

Preheat oven to 350° (or 325° for dark-coated metal pan). Position oven rack in middle of oven. Spray the bottom only of a 15 x 10 x 1-inch jelly roll pan with nonstick cooking spray (or foil-line pan; see page 11).

In a large bowl place the cake mix, mayonnaise, and eggs. Blend 2 minutes with an electric mixer set on medium speed until well blended and smooth. Stir in apples and dried cranberries. Pour and spread batter into prepared baking pan.

Bake 18–20 minutes or until toothpick inserted in center comes out clean. Transfer to wire rack and cool completely.

In a medium bowl beat the softened butter, powdered sugar, and lemon juice with electric mixer set on low speed 2 minutes. Beat on high speed until light and fluffy. Spread over cooled bars. Cut into bars. Store leftover bars in refrigerator.

Makes 36 large or 48 small bars.

Black-bottom Banana Cheesecake Bars

Looking for a stylish dessert to wrap up a casual summer gathering? You can both cool things down and fire things up when you pull these pretty (and very chocolate) cheesecake bars out of the icebox.

1	18.25-ounce package devil's food cake mix
3	8-ounce packages cream cheese, softened
3	large eggs
½	cup (1 stick) butter, melted
1	cup miniature semisweet chocolate chips
1	cup mashed ripe banana (about 2 large bananas)
1	cup powdered sugar, plus 1–2 tablespoons for garnish
1½	teaspoons vanilla extract

Preheat oven to 350° (or 325° for dark-coated metal pan). Position oven rack in middle of oven. Spray the bottom only of a 13 x 9-inch metal baking pan with nonstick cooking spray (or foil-line pan; see page 11).

In a large bowl place the cake mix, 4 ounces (half of one 8-ounce package) of the softened cream cheese, 1 of the eggs, and melted butter. Blend 2 minutes with an electric mixer set on low speed until well blended. Stir in chocolate chips. Press mixture into bottom of prepared pan.

Bake crust 15 minutes.

While crust bakes, in a medium bowl place the remaining cream cheese, mashed banana, 1 cup powdered sugar, and vanilla extract. Blend 2 minutes with electric mixer set on medium speed until blended and smooth. Add remaining 2 eggs, one at a time, beating only until incorporated. Spread cream cheese mixture evenly over chocolate crust.

Bake 25–28 minutes or until just set. Transfer to wire rack and cool completely. Refrigerate at least 2 hours before serving. Cut into bars and sprinkle with remaining 1–2 tablespoons powdered sugar.

Makes 24 large or 36 small bars.

Carmelitas

*Pick up a good book, brew a pot of coffee, and head
to your favorite easy chair with one of these carmelita bars in hand.
Don't forget the napkin as these treats are definitely on the
(deliciously) gooey side.*

1	18.25-ounce package yellow cake mix
1	cup (2 sticks) butter, melted
2	cups quick-cooking oats
2	cups miniature semisweet chocolate chips, divided
1	16-ounce container caramel apple dip

Preheat oven to 350° (or 325° for dark-coated metal pan). Position oven rack in middle of oven. Spray the bottom only of a 13 x 9-inch metal baking pan with nonstick cooking spray (or foil-line pan; see page 11).

Place the cake mix and melted butter in a large bowl. Blend 1–2 minutes with an electric mixer set on low speed until well blended. Stir in oats until blended. Press half of mixture evenly into prepared pan. Add 1 cup miniature chocolate chips to remaining mixture; set aside momentarily.

In a medium bowl stir together the caramel dip and remaining 1 cup chocolate chips. Pour caramel mixture over prepared crust and sprinkle with reserved crumb mixture.

Bake 28–30 minutes or until topping is firm to the touch. Transfer to a wire rack and cool completely. Cut into bars.

Makes 24 large or 36 small bars.

Mother Lode Chocolate Toffee Caramel Bars

It seems that something chocolate is nearly everyone's favorite dessert. These quick and easy bars, loaded with caramel, toffee, and even more chocolate, qualify as one such something, effortlessly.

1	18.25-ounce package yellow cake mix
⅓	cup vegetable oil
2	large eggs
1	cup semisweet chocolate chips
1	cup white chocolate chips
3	1.4-ounce chocolate-covered toffee candy bars, coarsely chopped
32	caramels, unwrapped
½	cup (1 stick) butter
1	14-ounce can sweetened condensed milk

Preheat oven to 350° (or 325° for dark-coated metal pan). Position oven rack in middle of oven. Spray the bottom only of a 13 x 9-inch metal baking pan with nonstick cooking spray (or foil-line pan; see page 11).

In a large bowl place the cake mix, oil, and eggs. Blend 2 minutes with an electric mixer set on medium speed until well blended. Stir in semisweet chocolate chips and white chocolate chips. Press half of mixture into bottom of prepared pan. Stir toffee pieces into remaining half.

Bake crust 10 minutes.

While the crust bakes, place the caramels, butter, and condensed milk in a medium heavy saucepan. Cook and stir over medium-low heat until caramels are melted and mixture is blended and smooth; pour evenly over partially baked crust and sprinkle with the remaining cake mix mixture.

Bake 25–28 minutes or until the topping is golden and firm to the touch. Transfer to wire rack. Run knife around edges of pan to loosen; cool completely.

Makes 24 large or 36 small bars.

Cinnamon-Raisin Walnut Bars

Cinnamon and spice are extra nice when accompanied by crunchy pecans and plump raisins in a quick cookie bar. For a tart contrast of flavors, substitute dried cranberries or tart dried cherries for the raisins.

1   **18.25-ounce package spice cake mix**
½   **cup (1 stick) butter, melted**
1   **large egg yolk**
1   **14-ounce can sweetened condensed milk**
1¼   **teaspoons ground cinnamon**
1½   **cups raisins**
1   **cup cinnamon baking chips**
1   **cup coarsely chopped walnuts (or pecans)**

Preheat oven to 350° (or 325° for dark-coated metal pan). Position oven rack in middle of oven. Spray the bottom only of a 13 x 9-inch metal baking pan with nonstick cooking spray (or foil-line pan; see page 11).

In a large bowl place the cake mix, melted butter, and egg yolk. Blend 1–2 minutes with an electric mixer set on low speed until well blended. Press mixture into prepared pan.

Bake crust 15 minutes.

Meanwhile, in a medium mixing bowl combine condensed milk, cinnamon, and raisins until blended. Spoon and spread mixture over hot crust. Sprinkle with cinnamon chips and nuts; gently press into condensed milk layer.

Bake 16–18 minutes longer or until lightly browned at edges. Transfer to a wire rack and cool completely. Cut into bars. Store loosely covered at room temperature.

Makes 24 large or 36 small bars.

Coconut-Pecan Chocolate Fudge Bars

Your most vivid chocolate fantasy, these bars walk a fine line between cookie and candy.

1	18.25-ounce package chocolate cake mix
¾	cup butter, melted
1	large egg
2½	cups quick-cooking oats
1	15-ounce tub coconut pecan frosting
2	cups semisweet chocolate chips
1	cup chopped pecans

Preheat oven to 350° for metal or glass pan. Position oven rack in middle of oven. Spray the bottom only of a 15 x 10 x 1-inch jelly roll pan with nonstick cooking spray (or foil-line pan; see page 11).

Reserve 3 tablespoons of the cake mix. In a large bowl place the remaining cake mix, melted butter, and egg. Blend 1–2 minutes with an electric mixer set on low speed until well blended. Stir in oats until blended. Press two-thirds of cake mix mixture (about 2½ cups) into bottom of prepared pan.

Place frosting in medium microwave-safe bowl; microwave on high for 1 minute. Add reserved 3 tablespoons cake mix; stir until well blended.

Drizzle half of frosting mixture over cake mix mixture in pan, spreading evenly. Sprinkle with chocolate chips and pecans. Drizzle with remaining frosting mixture. Crumble remaining cake mix mixture over frosting mixture.

Bake 25–30 minutes or until top is golden brown and edges are bubbly. Transfer to wire rack and cool completely.

Makes 36 large or 48 small bars.

Tri-level Mocha Cheesecake Bars

As luscious proof that decadent desserts can be quick and easy too, these delectable espresso-spiked chocolate treats come together in no time. A chocolate lover's delight, they will satisfy even the most intense chocolate cravings.

1   **18.25-ounce package chocolate cake mix**
½   **cup (1 stick) butter, melted**
3   **large eggs**
1   **tablespoon instant espresso or coffee powder**
3   **teaspoons vanilla extract, divided**
2   **8-ounce packages cream cheese, softened**
¾   **cup powdered sugar, divided**
1   **16-ounce container (2 cups) sour cream**

Preheat oven to 350° (or 325° for dark-coated metal pan). Position oven rack in middle of oven. Spray the bottom only of a 13 x 9-inch metal baking pan with nonstick cooking spray (or foil-line pan; see page 11).

In a large bowl place the cake mix, melted butter, and 1 of the eggs. Blend 1–2 minutes with an electric mixer set on low speed until well blended. Press mixture into prepared pan.

Bake 10 minutes. Remove from oven (leave oven on).

While crust bakes, in a medium bowl dissolve espresso powder in 2 teaspoons of the vanilla extract. Add the softened cream cheese and ½ cup of the powdered sugar to the same bowl and blend with electric mixer set on medium speed until well blended and smooth. Add remaining 2 eggs, one at a time, mixing on low speed after each addition just until blended. Pour over hot crust.

Bake 22–25 minutes or until center is just barely set when pan is jiggled (do not overbake); remove from oven (leave oven on).

In a large mixing bowl whisk the sour cream with the remaining ¼ cup powdered sugar and 1 teaspoon vanilla extract; spread evenly over bars. Return bars to oven for 5 minutes. Transfer to wire rack and cool completely. Refrigerate at least 4 hours or overnight. Cut into bars.

Makes 36 medium bars or 48 small squares.

Raspberry Swirl Sour Cream Bars

Spring is a season of celebrations. Start the party planning with these quick-to-prepare, but oh-so-impressive bars, perfect for receptions, showers, and graduation parties. Other jams and preserves can be substituted for the raspberry preserves. Consider apricot preserves, orange marmalade, or lemon curd.

1	18.25-ounce package vanilla cake mix
½	cup sour cream
⅓	cup butter, melted
1	teaspoon vanilla extract
2	large eggs
1	12-ounce jar seedless raspberry preserves, stirred to loosen

Preheat oven to 350° for metal or glass pan. Position oven rack in middle of oven. Spray the bottom only of a 13 x 9-inch pan with nonstick cooking spray (or foil-line pan; see page 11).

In a large bowl place the cake mix, sour cream, melted butter, vanilla extract, and eggs. Blend 2 minutes with an electric mixer set on medium speed until well blended. Reserve 1 cup of batter. Spread remaining batter into prepared pan. Distribute raspberry preserves evenly over batter. Drop remaining cake batter by tablespoonfuls over preserves. Swirl batter and jam with tip of knife.

Bake 23–26 minutes or until toothpick inserted near center comes out clean. Transfer to wire rack and cool completely.

Makes 36 large or 48 small bars.

Date Bars Deluxe

As a child I painstakingly picked out every date from the granola, trail mix, and gorp my mother offered up as snacks. I'm unsure of my reason, but I think it was because I did not like the look of them. So it came as a surprise to everyone when I went crazy for the date bars delivered on a neighbor's cookie plate one Christmas. Most likely my instant love affair stemmed from my failure to recognize that dates were involved. Date bars remain one of my favorite curl-up-with-a-cup-of-tea cookie options. Although simplified with cake mix, this version tastes nothing short of deluxe.

2½ cups water
½ cup fresh lemon juice
3 cups chopped pitted dates
2 teaspoons vanilla extract
1 18.25-ounce package yellow cake mix
1 teaspoon ground cinnamon
1 cup (2 sticks) butter, melted
2¼ cups quick-cooking oats

Combine water and lemon juice in a medium saucepan. Bring to a boil over medium heat. Add dates; simmer until very soft and thick, stirring occasionally, about 10 minutes. Cool to room temperature. Stir in vanilla extract.

Preheat oven to 350° (or 325° for dark-coated metal pan). Position oven rack in middle of oven. Spray the bottom only of a 13 x 9-inch baking pan with nonstick cooking spray (or foil-line pan; see page 11).

In a large bowl place the cake mix, cinnamon, and melted butter. Blend 1–2 minutes with an electric mixer set on medium speed until well blended and smooth. Stir in the oats until blended. Press half of mixture evenly into prepared pan.

Spoon and spread date mixture over prepared crust; top with reserved crumb mixture and press down gently.

Bake 30–34 minutes or until topping is firm to the touch. Transfer to wire rack and cool completely.

Makes 24 large or 36 small bars.

Peppermint White Chocolate Cheesecake Bars

The weather outside may be frightful, but your kitchen will be delightful
if you bake up these cool mint-y bars come holiday-time.
To crush the candies, place in a heavy-duty zippered plastic bag
and bang with a rolling pin or can (it doubles as holiday stress relief).

1	18.25-ounce package vanilla cake mix
½	cup (1 stick) butter, melted
3	large eggs
3	8-ounce packages cream cheese, softened
⅔	cup sugar
1¼	teaspoons peppermint extract
2	cups white chocolate chips
2	teaspoons vegetable shortening
1	cup coarsely crushed red & white striped peppermint candies or candy canes

Preheat oven to 350° (or 325° for dark-coated metal pan). Position oven rack in middle of oven. Spray the bottom only of a 13 x 9-inch metal baking pan with nonstick cooking spray (or foil-line pan; see page 11).

In a large bowl place the cake mix, melted butter, and 1 of the eggs. Blend 1–2 minutes with an electric mixer set on low speed until well blended. Press mixture evenly into prepared pan.

Bake crust 15 minutes.

While crust bakes, in a large mixing bowl beat the softened cream cheese and sugar with electric mixer set on high speed until blended and smooth. Gradually beat in remaining 2 eggs, one at a time, and peppermint extract until smooth. Stir in 1 cup of the white chocolate chips. Pour over partially baked crust.

Bake 23–36 minutes, until just barely set at center (do not overbake). Transfer to a wire rack and cool completely.

In heavy saucepan melt remaining 1 cup white chocolate chips with shortening until smooth; drizzle over cooled bars. Immediately sprinkle with crushed peppermint candies. Chill at least 3 hours in refrigerator. Cut into bars. Store in refrigerator.

Variation:

Dark Chocolate Peppermint Cheesecake Bars: Prepare as directed above but use chocolate or devil's food cake mix in place of the vanilla cake mix and semisweet chocolate chips in place of the white chocolate chips.

Makes 24 large or 36 small bars.

New York Cheesecake Bars

Forget the springform pan—you can make an incredible, New York–style cheesecake in a plain 13x9-inch baking pan. Not only is it a breeze to make, it is much easier to cut and serve to a crowd—or a small army. Because this silky-rich cheesecake is skyscraper-high, one square will go a long way. For a dressed-up dessert, serve the squares plated with a drizzle of chocolate or caramel sauce, fresh fruit, or a quick berry compote. And for an easy flavor variation, vary the cake mix for the crust. Lemon, chocolate, and spice cake are particularly delicious.

1	18.25-ounce package vanilla cake mix
½	cup (1 stick) butter, melted
4	large eggs
3	8-ounce packages cream cheese, softened
1¾	cups powdered sugar, divided
3	teaspoons vanilla extract, divided
1	16-ounce container (2 cups) sour cream

Preheat oven to 350° (or 325° for dark-coated metal pan). Position oven rack in middle of oven. Spray the bottom only of a 13 x 9-inch metal baking pan with nonstick cooking spray (or foil-line pan; see page 11).

Place the cake mix, melted butter and 1 egg in a large bowl. Blend 1–2 minutes with an electric mixer set on low speed until well blended. Press mixture evenly into prepared pan. Bake crust 15 minutes.

While crust bakes, beat softened cream cheese, 1¼ cups of the powdered sugar, and 2 teaspoons of the vanilla extract with electric mixer set on medium speed until well blended, scraping down bowl several times. Add remaining 3 eggs, one at a time, mixing on low speed after each addition just until blended. Pour over hot crust.

Bake 23–26 minutes or until center is just barely set when pan is jiggled (do not overbake); remove from oven (leave oven on).

In a large mixing bowl whisk the sour cream with the remaining ½ cup powdered sugar and 1 teaspoon vanilla extract; spread evenly over bars. Return bars to oven for 5 minutes. Transfer to wire rack and cool completely. Refrigerate at least 4 hours or overnight. Cut into bars.

Variation:

Fresh Berry Cheesecake Bars: Prepare as directed above but eliminate the final sour cream topping steps. Instead, distribute 2 cups fresh raspberries, blackberries, or blueberries over the cheesecake batter before baking. Sprinkle the cooled, chilled bars with powdered sugar.

Makes 36 medium bars or 48 small squares.

Brown Sugar–Milk Chocolate Meringue Bars

Growing up, I loved lemon meringue pie, but only the lemon filling and crust—I thought the puffy meringue was some sort of penance for an otherwise heavenly dessert. Some years later, I had my first crisp meringue at a neighborhood bakery. Crisp and crunchy—it was nothing like the seepy version I was used to, and I was instantly hooked. These bars have the same crispy meringue, made even better with brown sugar, wrapped around a milk chocolate and almond filling.

1   18.25-ounce package German chocolate cake mix
½   cup (1 stick) butter, melted
2   large egg yolks
1   12-ounce package (2 cups) milk chocolate chips
1   cup sliced almonds, divided
4   large egg whites, room temperature
1   cup packed dark brown sugar

Preheat oven to 375°(or 350° for dark-coated metal pan). Position oven rack in middle of oven. Spray the bottom only of a 13 x 9-inch metal baking pan with nonstick cooking spray (or foil-line pan; see page 11).

In a large bowl place the cake mix, melted butter, and egg yolks. Blend 1–2 minutes with an electric mixer set on low speed until well blended. Press mixture evenly into prepared pan.

Bake crust 20 minutes. Remove pan from oven (leave oven on). Sprinkle with chocolate chips and ½ cup of the almonds. Transfer to wire rack while preparing meringue.

In a large mixing bowl beat the egg whites with an electric mixer set on high until frothy. Gradually add brown sugar; beat until stiff peaks form. Carefully spread meringue over chips and nuts. Sprinkle with remaining ½ cup almonds.

Bake an additional 13–15 minutes or until meringue is golden brown. Transfer to a wire rack and cool completely. Cut into bars.

Variation:

Dark Chocolate–Raspberry Meringue Bars: Prepare as directed above but use semisweet chocolate chips in place of the milk chocolate chips and eliminate the almonds. After sprinkling crust with chocolate chips, dollop ½ cup seedless raspberry preserves, in teaspoons, over the chips. Use plain white granulated sugar in place of the brown sugar in the meringue.

Makes 24 large or 36 small bars.

Lemon Curd Swirl Cheesecake Bars

A swirl of purchased lemon curd makes all the difference in these simple-to-make, elegant bars. Serve them at your next summertime get-together and let the kudos resound.

1	18.25-ounce package lemon cake mix
½	cup (1 stick) butter, melted
1	tablespoon grated lemon zest
3	large eggs
2	8-ounce packages cream cheese, softened
⅓	cup sugar
1	tablespoon fresh lemon juice
2	tablespoons all-purpose flour
1	12-ounce jar lemon curd, room temperature

Preheat oven to 350° (or 325° for dark-coated metal pan). Position oven rack in middle of oven. Spray the bottom only of a 13 x 9-inch baking pan with nonstick cooking spray (or foil-line pan; see page 11).

In a large bowl place the cake mix, melted butter, lemon zest, and 1 of the eggs. Blend 1–2 minutes with an electric mixer set on medium speed until well blended. Press into prepared pan.

Bake 15 minutes. Remove from oven (leave oven on).

While the crust bakes, place the softened cream cheese and sugar in same large bowl (no need to clean). Blend with an electric mixer set on medium speed until light and fluffy. Add the lemon juice and flour; beat until smooth, scraping down sides with rubber spatula. Beat in remaining 2 eggs, one at a time, until blended. Spread cream cheese mixture evenly over crust. Distribute the lemon curd in spoonfuls evenly over the cream cheese layer. Swirl the lemon curd & cream cheese batter with tip of a knife.

Bake bars in middle of oven for 23–26 minutes or until topping is just barely set when the pan is jiggled (do not overbake). Transfer to a wire rack and cool completely. Chill in refrigerator at least 3 hours or until firm. Cut into bars or squares.

Makes 24 large or 36 small bars.

Toffee Cream Cheese Streusel Bars

I do not trust myself alone with these bars. Loaded with brown sugar, cream cheese, and toffee, they are everything a favorite bar cookie should be: simple to make and splendid to eat.

1   18.25-ounce package yellow cake mix
¼   cup packed dark brown sugar
1   cup (2 sticks) butter, melted
2¼   cups quick-cooking oats
2   8-ounce packages cream cheese, softened
½   cup packed light brown sugar
1½   teaspoons vanilla extract
2   large eggs
1   cup toffee baking bits, divided

Preheat oven to 350° (or 325° for dark-coated metal pan). Position oven rack in middle of oven. Spray the bottom only of a 13 x 9-inch metal baking pan with nonstick cooking spray (or foil-line pan; see page 11).

In a large bowl place the cake mix, ¼ cup dark brown sugar, and melted butter. Blend 1–2 minutes with an electric mixer set on medium speed until well blended and smooth. Stir in oats. Press half of mixture evenly into prepared pan.

In a large mixing bowl beat the softened cream cheese and ½ cup light brown sugar with electric mixer set on high speed until smooth. Add vanilla extract and eggs, one at a time; beat until just blended. Stir in ½ cup toffee bits. Spoon and spread cream cheese mixture over base layer. Add remaining ½ cup toffee bits to remaining crumb mixture; sprinkle over cream cheese layer and press down gently.

Bake 30–34 minutes or until topping is golden and firm to the touch. Transfer to wire rack and cool completely.

Makes 24 large or 36 small bars.

Caramel Rocky Road Bars

Sometimes mistakes are wonderful. Case in point, these bars, which were originally supposed to have chocolate fudge topping. But when I asked a friend to pick up the ingredients to test these one day, she came back with caramel. I decided "what the heck" and gave it a try. What a treat! They are favorites wherever they go. Any caramel topping will do, but for a truly amazing bar, buy a premium brand.

1½	cups lightly salted peanuts, divided
1	18.25-ounce package devils food cake mix
1	cup (2 sticks) butter, melted
2¼	cups quick-cooking oats
1	17.5-ounce jar caramel ice cream topping
4	cups miniature marshmallows
1½	cups semisweet chocolate chips

Preheat oven to 350° (or 325° for dark-coated metal pan). Position oven rack in middle of oven. Spray the bottom only of a 13 x 9-inch metal baking pan with nonstick cooking spray (or foil-line pan; see page 11).

Coarsely chop ½ cup of the peanuts. In a large bowl place the chopped peanuts, cake mix, and melted butter. Blend 1–2 minutes with an electric mixer set on medium speed until well blended. Stir in oats until blended. Press half of mixture evenly into prepared pan.

Pour caramel topping evenly over crust. Sprinkle with marshmallows, remaining 1 cup peanuts, and chocolate chips. Top with reserved oat mixture; press down gently.

Bake 30–34 minutes or until topping is set and firm to the touch. Transfer to wire rack and cool completely.

Makes 24 large or 36 small bars.

Fresh Cranberry–Caramel Streusel Bars

You know that cookie on the Christmas cookie plate that everyone fights over?
This is it. You may not have considered the combination of cranberry and caramel before
now, but you'll never forget it after tasting these rich treats. They are definitely
holiday fare, but if you stow a few bags of fresh cranberries in the freezer,
you can make and enjoy them year-round.

1	18.25-ounce package yellow cake mix
1	cup (2 sticks) butter, melted
2⅓	cups quick-cooking oats
1	12-ounce jar caramel ice cream topping
1	10-ounce package chopped dates
1⅓	cups chopped fresh cranberries
¾	cup chopped pecans

Preheat oven to 350° (or 325° for dark-coated metal pan). Position oven rack in middle of oven. Spray the bottom only of a 13 x 9-inch metal baking pan with nonstick cooking spray (or foil-line pan; see page 11).

Set aside ⅓ cup cake mix. In a large bowl place the remaining cake mix and melted butter. Blend 1–2 minutes with an electric mixer set on medium speed until well blended and smooth. Stir in oats until blended. Press half of mixture evenly into prepared pan.

In a medium bowl whisk the caramel topping and reserved ⅓ cup cake mix until blended; mix in the dates and cranberries. Spoon and spread the caramel mixture over prepared crust; top with reserved crumb mixture and pecans and press down gently.

Bake 30–34 minutes or until topping is firm to the touch. Transfer to wire rack and cool completely.

Makes 24 large or 36 small bars.

Butterscotch Blondies

The brownie has legions of loyal fans, but the blondie has a multitude of equally stead-fast enthusiasts. The reasons are clear: a rich and chewy butterscotch bar, studded with more butterscotch or a contrast of chocolate chips, and highly transportable to boot.

1	18.25-ounce package yellow cake mix
¼	cup packed dark brown sugar
2	large eggs
½	cup (1 stick) butter, melted
1	teaspoon vanilla extract
1	cup semisweet chocolate chips or butterscotch baking chips
1	cup chopped pecans, optional

Preheat oven to 350°. Position oven rack in center of oven. Set aside a 13 x 9-inch baking pan.

In a large mixing bowl blend the cake mix, brown sugar, eggs, melted butter, and vanilla extract with electric mixer on low speed until all dry ingredients are moistened, about 1–2 minutes. Mix in the chocolate chips or butterscotch chips (dough will be stiff).

Spoon the dough into the ungreased 13x9-inch pan; spread dough evenly with rubber spatula or fingers (dough will puff and spread as it bakes). If desired, sprinkle with chopped pecans; gently press into dough.

Bake 22–25 minutes or until the bars are golden brown but still soft. Transfer pan to a wire rack and cool completely. Cut into bars or squares.

Variations:

Apple Blondies with Caramel Frosting: Prepare as directed above but substitute 1 cup peeled, chopped tart apple (about 1 large) for the chocolate chips (pecans are still optional). Frost cooled blondies with Caramel Frosting (see page 211).

White Chocolate Blondies: Prepare as directed above but eliminate the brown sugar, substitute vanilla cake mix for the yellow cake mix, use white chocolate chips in place of semisweet chocolate chips, and use ½ teaspoon almond extract in place of the vanilla extract. If nuts are desired, substitute an equal amount of sliced or slivered almonds for the pecans.

Makes 24 large or 36 small bars or squares.

Peanut Butter Blondies

Can the butterscotch blondie be made better? For peanut butter fiends, the answer is a resounding yes and involves merely stirring some peanut butter into the batter. Delicious!

1   18.25-ounce package yellow cake mix
⅓   cup butter, melted
2   large eggs
3   teaspoons vanilla extract, divided
⅔   cup plus 1 tablespoon creamy peanut butter (not natural style), divided
1   cup powdered sugar
2–3 tablespoons milk

Preheat oven to 350° (or 325° for dark-coated metal pan). Position oven rack in middle of oven. Set aside a 13 x 9-inch baking pan.

In a large bowl mix the cake mix, melted butter, eggs and 1 teaspoon vanilla extract with an electric mixer on low speed for 30 seconds. Stop the mixer and scrape down the sides of the bowl. Increase the mixer speed to medium and beat 1 to 2 minutes more or until batter is smooth and very thick. Stir in ⅔ cup peanut butter with a wooden spoon.

Spoon the dough into the ungreased 13 x 9-inch pan; spread evenly with rubber spatula or fingers (dough will puff and spread as it bakes).

Bake 22–25 minutes until just set at center (do not overbake). Transfer to a wire rack and cool completely.

In a small bowl whisk the powdered sugar, remaining teaspoon vanilla extract and remaining tablespoon peanut butter until blended, adding enough milk to make drizzling consistency; drizzle over cooled bars. Cut into bars or squares.

Variations:

Chocolate-Chip Peanut Butter Blondies: Prepare as directed above but add 1 cup semisweet or milk chocolate chips to the batter along with the peanut butter.

Peanut Butter Blondies Deluxe: Prepare as directed above but add 1 cup peanut butter baking chips to the batter along with the peanut butter. After drizzling blondies with icing, sprinkle with ⅔ cup chopped peanuts.

Makes 24 large or 36 small bars.

Peanut Butter Blondies

Irish Cream Swirled Bars

*Not only are these liqueur-rich bars incredible and incredibly rich,
the recipe can be used as a template for countless variations,
depending on the cake mix, frosting, and spirits used.*

1	18.25-ounce package vanilla cake mix
3	large eggs
⅔	cup plus ¼ cup Irish Cream liqueur, divided
⅓	cup vegetable oil
1	16-ounce container cream cheese frosting
1½	cups white chocolate chips

Preheat oven to 350°. Position oven rack in middle of oven. Spray the bottom only of a 15 x 10 x 1-inch jelly roll pan with nonstick cooking spray (or foil-line pan; see page 11).

In a large bowl place the cake mix, eggs, ⅔ cup liqueur, and oil. Blend 1–2 minutes with an electric mixer set on low speed until well blended and smooth. Reserve ½ cup batter; spread remaining batter into bottom of prepared pan.

In same large bowl used for cake batter (no need to clean it) place the frosting, remaining ¼ cup liqueur, and reserved cake batter. Blend 1–2 minutes with an electric mixer (no need to clean beaters) set on low speed until well blended and smooth; stir in white chocolate chips. Drop large spoonfuls of this mixture over the cake batter. Swirl with tip of knife to make a marble effect.

Bake 24–27 minutes, or until the bars are just set and golden. Transfer pan to a wire rack and cool completely. Cut into bars or squares.

Variation:
Chocolate Whiskey Swirl Bars: Prepare as directed above but use chocolate cake mix in place of vanilla cake mix, chocolate cream cheese frosting in place of cream cheese frosting, whiskey in place of Irish Cream liqueur, and semisweet chocolate chips in place of white chocolate chips.

Makes 48 bars or squares.

Peanut Butter Cup Caramel Bars

Peanut butter, chocolate, caramel, cake, and frosting in one bar cookie?
Gooey-licious.

1   18.25-ounce package yellow or chocolate cake mix
½   cup (1 stick) butter, softened
2   large eggs
20 miniature peanut butter cups, chopped
2   tablespoons cornstarch
1   12-ounce jar caramel ice cream topping
¼   cup creamy peanut butter
1   cup lightly salted, coarsely chopped peanuts, divided
1   recipe Milk Chocolate Frosting (see page 209)

Preheat oven to 350° (or 325° for dark-coated metal pan). Position oven rack in middle of oven. Spray the bottom only of a 13 x 9-inch metal baking pan with nonstick cooking spray (or foil-line pan; see page 11).

In a large bowl place the cake mix, softened butter, and eggs. Blend with an electric mixer 1–2 minutes on medium speed until all dry ingredients are moistened and mixture is well blended. Stir in the peanut butter cups. Spread mixture evenly into the prepared pan.

Bake 18–22 minutes or until golden brown.

Meanwhile, in a medium saucepan combine cornstarch, caramel topping, and peanut butter, stirring until smooth. Cook and continue to stir over low heat until mixture begins to bubble.

Remove from heat and stir in ½ cup of the peanuts; spread evenly over warm crust.

Bake 5 minutes longer. Transfer to wire rack and cool completely.

Prepare Milk Chocolate Frosting. Spread bars with frosting and sprinkle with remaining ½ cup peanuts. Refrigerate for at least an hour before cutting. Cut into bars. Store in the refrigerator.

Makes 24 large or 36 small bars.

Chocolate-Covered Pretzel Bars

Everyone who loves the combination of salty and sweet will think these bars are brilliant.

1	18.25-ounce package German chocolate cake mix
½	cup (1 stick) butter, melted
1	large egg
⅔	cup crushed pretzels
1	cup semisweet chocolate chips
1	cup butterscotch baking chips
1	cup flaked coconut
1	cup coarsely chopped lightly salted mixed nuts
1	14-ounce can sweetened condensed milk

Preheat oven to 350° (or 325° for dark-coated metal pan). Position oven rack in middle of oven. Spray the bottom only of a 13 x 9-inch metal baking pan with nonstick cooking spray (or foil-line pan; see page 11).

In a large bowl place the cake mix, melted butter, and egg. Blend with an electric mixer 1–2 minutes on medium speed until all dry ingredients are moistened and mixture is well blended. Stir in pretzels. Press pretzel mixture into bottom of prepared pan.

Bake crust 15 minutes.

Layer the chocolate chips, butterscotch chips, coconut and nuts over crust; drizzle with condensed milk.

Bake 25–28 minutes or until edges are golden brown. Transfer to wire rack and cool completely before cutting into bars.

Makes 24 large or 36 small bars.

Toasted Almond Buttermilk Bars

The toasted almonds are a delicious, crunchy counterpoint to the creamy buttermilk custard in these home-style bars.

1   18.25-ounce package vanilla cake mix
½   cup (1 stick) butter, softened
1   3-ounce package cream cheese, softened
2   cups packed light brown sugar
1½   cups buttermilk (not nonfat)
4   large eggs
½   cup (1 stick) butter, melted
⅓   cup all-purpose flour
2   teaspoons vanilla extract
2   cups sliced almonds
2–3 tablespoons powdered sugar

Preheat oven to 350°. Position oven rack in middle of oven. Set aside an ungreased 15 x 10 x 1-inch jelly roll pan.

In a large bowl place the cake mix, softened butter, and cream cheese. Blend 2 minutes with an electric mixer set on low speed until blended and a crumbly dough forms. Gather dough together and press into jelly roll pan.

Bake crust 10 minutes.

Meanwhile, in a large bowl place the brown sugar, buttermilk, eggs, ½ cup melted butter, flour, and vanilla extract and mix with an electric mixer set on low speed until well blended. Stir in almonds. Pour mixture over partially baked crust.

Bake 25–28 minutes or until golden brown and firm to the touch. Transfer to wire rack and cool completely before cutting into squares. Sprinkle cooled squares with powered sugar.

Makes 48 bars.

Rosemary-Walnut Shortbread Squares

Begin brewing the Earl Grey and Darjeeling—this is one sophisticated tea-time nibble. Be sure to use white cake mix here—it has less fat than other cake mixes, producing just the right consistency.

1	18.25-ounce package white cake mix
½	cup (1 stick) butter, softened
1	3-ounce package cream cheese, softened
1	tablespoon fresh chopped rosemary or 1½ teaspoons dried crumbled rosemary
1	large egg white, room temperature
1	teaspoon vanilla extract
2	tablespoons powdered sugar
1	cup finely chopped walnuts

Preheat oven to 350°. Position oven rack in middle of oven. Set aside an ungreased 15 x 10 x 1-inch jelly roll pan.

Place the cake mix, butter, cream cheese and rosemary in a large bowl. Blend 1–2 minutes with electric mixer set on low speed until a crumbly dough forms. Gather dough together and press into jelly roll pan.

Clean the beaters on the electric mixer. In small bowl beat the egg white with vanilla and powdered sugar with electric mixer set on high speed until stiff peaks form.

Spread dough with egg white mixture; sprinkle with walnuts. Bake 15–18 minutes until golden brown and firm to the touch. Cool completely before cutting into squares.

Variations:

Orange-Almond Shortbread: Prepare as directed above but substitute 1 tablespoon grated orange zest for the rosemary, ½ teaspoon almond extract for the vanilla extract, and 1 cup finely chopped almonds for the walnuts.

Brown Sugar–Pecan Shortbread: Prepare as directed above but eliminate the rosemary, add ¼ cup firmly packed dark brown sugar to the cake mix dough, and substitute 1 cup finely chopped pecans for the walnuts.

Makes 48 cookies.

Blueberry Sour Cream Kuchen Bars

As the name implies, these easily assembled bars are inspired by German kuchen (pronounced KOO-khehn), which is a cheese- or fruit-filled bread that can be eaten for breakfast or dessert. The blueberries can be substituted with your favorite fruit of choice, from apricots to apples to fresh or frozen peaches.

1	18.25-ounce package yellow cake mix
½	cup (1 stick) butter, softened
1	3-ounce package cream cheese, softened
2	large eggs
2	cups sour cream (not reduced fat)
¼	cup sugar
½	teaspoon cinnamon
2	cups fresh or frozen (thawed) blueberries

Preheat oven to 350°. Position oven rack in middle of oven. Set aside an ungreased 13 x 9-inch baking pan.

In a large bowl place the cake mix, softened butter, cream cheese, and 1 of the eggs. Blend with electric mixer 1–2 minutes on low speed until a dough forms. Gather dough together and press into ungreased pan.

Bake crust 10–12 minutes or until light golden.

In a medium bowl whisk the sour cream with the sugar, cinnamon, and remaining egg until blended and smooth; mix in the blueberries. Spread mixture over partially baked crust.

Bake for 13–15 minutes, until sour cream layer is just set. Transfer to a wire rack and cool completely. Cut into bars. Store, covered, in refrigerator.

Makes 36 small or 24 large bars.

Double Berry Streusel Bars

Looking for the perfect picnic bar cookie? Look no further. Loaded with the flavor of blueberries, raspberries, and the zing of fresh lemon peel, they taste like summer.

1	18.25-ounce package yellow cake mix
1	cup (2 sticks) butter, melted
2¼	cups quick-cooking oats
1	12-ounce package frozen (thawed) blueberries
¾	cup seedless raspberry jam
1	tablespoon grated lemon zest

Preheat oven to 350° (or 325° for dark-coated metal pan). Position oven rack in middle of oven. Spray the bottom only of a 13 x 9-inch metal baking pan with nonstick cooking spray (or foil-line pan; see page 11).

Set aside 3 tablespoons of the cake mix. Place the remaining cake mix and melted butter in a large bowl. Blend 1–2 minutes with an electric mixer set on low speed until blended and smooth. Stir in oats until blended. Press half of mixture evenly into prepared pan.

In a large mixing bowl stir together the blueberries, jam, reserved 3 tablespoons cake mix, and lemon zest. Spoon and spread berry mixture over prepared crust; top with reserved crumb mixture and press down gently.

Bake 30–34 minutes or until topping is set and firm to the touch. Transfer to wire rack and cool completely.

Makes 24 large or 36 small bars.

Caramel Apple Streusel Bars

Surprise your favorite apple aficionado with these caramel apple bars to convey the extent of your good wishes.

1   18.25-ounce package yellow cake mix
1   cup (2 sticks) butter, melted
2¼ cups quick-cooking oats
4   cups coarsely chopped, peeled tart apples (about 4 apples)
1   16-ounce container caramel apple dip

Preheat oven to 350° (or 325° for dark-coated metal pan). Position oven rack in middle of oven. Spray the bottom only of a 13 x 9-inch metal baking pan with nonstick cooking spray (or foil-line pan; see page 11).

Reserve 3 tablespoons cake mix. Place the remaining cake mix and melted butter in a large bowl. Blend 1–2 minutes with an electric mixer set on low speed until blended and smooth. Stir in oats until blended. Press half of mixture evenly into prepared pan.

In another large mixing bowl toss together the chopped apples and remaining 3 tablespoons cake mix; spread over prepared crust; set aside momentarily. Pour caramel dip evenly over apples. Top with reserved crumb mixture and press down gently.

Bake 30–34 minutes or until topping is set and firm to the touch. Transfer to wire rack and cool completely.

Variation:
Peachy Keen Streusel Bars: Prepare as directed above but substitute chopped fresh (or frozen, thawed) peaches for the apples and 1 12-ounce jar peach preserves for the caramel apple dip.

Makes 24 large or 36 small bars.

THREE

Shaped and Filled Cookies

"Have It Your Way" Cake Mix Cookies

This recipe is my very favorite template cookie—it can be varied in countless ways depending on the flavor of cake mix and choice of add-ins. You can add 1 cup of any of the options below or mix it up and add a combination of add-ins (e.g., ½ cup milk chips and ½ cup coconut or ½ cup dried cranberries and ½ cup chopped pecans). Let your imagination be your guide!

1   18.25-ounce package cake mix, any flavor
½   cup (1 stick) butter, softened
2   large eggs
⅔   cup quick-cooking oats
1   cup of any of the following options:
   - chocolate chips or chunks (semisweet, milk, bittersweet, white)
   - baking chips (cinnamon, butterscotch, peanut butter)
   - toffee baking bits
   - sweetened flaked coconut
   - dried fruit
   - chopped nuts (any variety)

Preheat oven to 350°. Position oven rack in middle of oven. Spray cookie sheets with nonstick cooking spray.

In a large mixing bowl place half of the cake mix along with the softened butter and eggs. Blend with an electric mixer set on medium-high speed 1–2 minutes, until blended and smooth. Stir in the remaining cake mix, oats and stir-in(s) of choice (1 cup total) with a wooden spoon until all dry ingredients are moistened.

Roll dough into 1-inch balls; place 2 inches apart on prepared sheets. Flatten balls slightly with bottom of glass.

Bake 8–10 minutes or until edges are firm and center is just barely set when lightly touched. Cool 3 minutes on sheets. Transfer to wire racks with metal spatula and cool completely.

Makes about 3 dozen cookies.

Lemon-Lime Sugar Cookies

Bright with a double dose of citrus, these very easy, very citrus-y cookies are hands-down winners. Be sure to use real butter for optimal results.

¾ **cup (1½ sticks) butter, softened**
1 **large egg**
2 **tablespoons grated lime zest**
1 **18.25-ounce package lemon cake mix with pudding in the mix**
1 **cup yellow cornmeal**
½ **cup coarse sugar or granulated sugar for rolling**

Preheat oven to 375°. Position oven rack in middle of oven. Set aside ungreased cookie sheets.

In a large bowl beat the softened butter, egg, and lime zest on high speed until blended, about 1 minute. Gradually mix in the cake mix until blended and all dry ingredients are incorporated. Stir in the cornmeal by hand (dough will be stiff).

Place sugar in a shallow dish. Shape dough into 1-inch balls; roll in sugar to coat. Position 2 inches apart on ungreased cookie sheets.

Bake 9–10 minutes or until just set and bottoms are lightly browned. Remove from oven and let cool on sheets 1 minute. Transfer cookies to a wire rack with a metal spatula and cool completely.

Variations:

Lemon-Rosemary or Lemon-Thyme Sugar Cookies: Prepare as directed above but replace the lime zest with 2 tablespoons lemon zest and add 1 tablespoon chopped fresh rosemary or thyme leaves to the dough.

Double-Lime Sugar Cookies: Prepare as directed above but use vanilla cake mix. Prepare Lime Icing (see page 213) and drizzle over cooled cookies.

Orange Sugar Cookies: Prepare as directed above but use orange flavor or yellow cake mix and 2 tablespoons grated orange zest in place of the lime zest.

Vanilla Sugar Cookies: Prepare as directed above but use vanilla cake mix and 2 teaspoons vanilla extract in place of the lime zest.

Makes 3½ dozen cookies.

Pecan Sandies

¾ cup (1½ sticks) butter, softened
1 large egg
2 teaspoons vanilla extract
1 18.25-ounce package yellow cake mix with pudding in the mix
1¼ cups very finely chopped pecans
½ cup coarse sugar or granulated sugar for rolling

Preheat oven to 375°. Position oven rack in middle of oven. Set aside ungreased cookie sheets.

In a large bowl beat the butter, egg, and vanilla extract on high speed until blended, about 1 minute. Gradually mix in the cake mix until blended and all dry ingredients are incorporated. Stir in the pecans by hand (dough will be stiff).

Place sugar in a shallow dish. Shape dough into 1-inch balls; roll in sugar to coat. Position balls 2 inches apart on ungreased cookie sheets.

Bake 9–10 minutes or until just set and bottoms are lightly browned. Remove from oven and let cool on sheets 1 minute. Transfer cookies to a wire rack with a metal spatula and cool completely.

Variations:
Almond Sandies: Prepare as directed above but substitute finely chopped almonds for the pecans and replace the vanilla extract with ¾ teaspoon almond extract.

Peanut Brittle Sandies: Prepare as directed above but substitute finely chopped peanuts for the pecans. Just before baking, roll dough balls in toffee baking bits (you will need 1 10-ounce package).

Makes 3½ dozen cookies.

Snickery Hidden Treasure Cookies

These cookies are so easy and so delicious—and you can "hide" just about any variety of chocolate candy bar inside the dough. Do be sure to cool the cookies before eating to avoid burning tender tongues on the hot filling.

1   **18.25-ounce package yellow cake mix**
2   **large eggs**
⅓   **cup vegetable oil**
1   **bag mini-size chocolate-covered caramel nougat candy bar pieces**
       (e.g., Snickers®), unwrapped

Preheat oven to 400°. Position oven rack in middle of oven. Set aside an ungreased cookie sheet.

In a large bowl place half of the cake mix along with the eggs and oil. Blend with an electric mixer set on medium-high speed 1–2 minutes, until blended. Stir in the remaining cake mix until all dry ingredients are moistened.

Cut candy bars in half to create square-shaped pieces. Shape dough into 1½ inch balls. Place a candy bar half into the center of a ball of dough, shaping the dough around the candy to cover completely.

Place dough balls 2 inches apart on ungreased cookie sheet.

Bake 9–11 minutes or until dough is just set. Transfer to a wire rack and cool completely.

Variation:
Peanut Butter Cup Cookies: Prepare as directed above but use chocolate cake mix in place of yellow cake mix and miniature peanut butter cups in place of chocolate caramel nougat candies.

Makes about 3 dozen cookies.

Marbled Chocolate & Vanilla Cookies

With a gorgeous presentation and the rich, classic flavor combination of chocolate and vanilla, these cookies are showstoppers.

1	18.25-ounce package white cake mix
⅔	cup vegetable oil, divided
8	tablespoons (1 stick) butter, melted, divided
2	large eggs
3	teaspoons vanilla extract, divided
1	18.25-ounce package devil's food cake mix
1½	cups toasted pecans (or walnuts), divided

Preheat oven to 400°. Position oven rack in middle of oven. Set aside an ungreased cookie sheet.

In a large bowl place half of the white cake mix along with ⅓ cup oil, 4 table-spoons melted butter, 1 egg, and 1 teaspoon vanilla. Blend with an electric mixer set on medium speed 1–2 minutes, until blended. Stir in the remaining cake mix and ¾ cup of the nuts.

In a second large bowl place half of the devil's food cake mix, remaining ⅓ cup oil, remaining 4 tablespoons melted butter, remaining egg, and remaining 2 teaspoons vanilla extract. Blend with an electric mixer set on medium speed 1–2 minutes, until blended. Stir in the remaining cake mix and ¾ cup nuts.

Scoop 1 teaspoon of vanilla dough into ball. Scoop 1 teaspoon of chocolate dough into ball. Gently press dough balls together, then roll gently to form one ball. Place balls 2 inches apart on the ungreased cookie sheet.

Bake 10 minutes or just until cookies begin to brown (be careful not to overbake). Cool cookies on cookie sheets for 2 minutes. Transfer cookies to cooling racks and cool completely. Repeat with remaining chocolate and vanilla dough.

Variations:

Mocha Chip Marble Cookies: Prepare as directed above but dissolve 1 tablespoon instant espresso or coffee powder in the 1 teaspoon vanilla before adding to the white cake mix and substitute 1½ cups miniature semisweet chocolate chips for the chopped nuts.

Lemon Macadamia Marble Cookies: Prepare as directed above but use lemon cake mix in place of devil's food cake mix, substitute 3 teaspoons grated lemon zest for the vanilla extract, and use roasted, lightly salted chopped macadamia nuts instead of walnuts or pecans.

Makes 6 dozen cookies.

Strawberry–Cream Cheese Thumbprints

These sweet cookies are pretty-as-a-picture perfect, as welcome in a lunchbox as they are at a bridal shower. You can use the basic dough as a blueprint for your own thumbprint designs, varying the cake mix flavor and filling choice in endless permutations.

1   18.25-ounce package white cake mix
1   cup all-purpose flour
¼   cup (½ stick) butter, softened
1   3-ounce package cream cheese, softened
2   large egg yolks
1   teaspoon almond extract
⅔   cup strawberry jam, stirred to loosen

Preheat oven to 350°. Position oven rack to upper third of the oven. Set aside two ungreased cookie sheets.

In a large bowl place the cake mix, flour, softened butter, and cream cheese. Blend 1–2 minutes with an electric mixer set on low speed until mixture is blended and resembles fresh bread crumbs. Add the egg yolks and almond extract; beat on low speed 1–2 minutes longer until dough comes together into a ball.

Shape dough into 1-inch balls and position 2 inches apart on cookie sheets. Push an indentation into the center of each cookie with your thumb, the back of a rounded ¼-teaspoon measuring spoon, or cork. Fill each indentation with ¼ teaspoon jam.

Bake 8–10 minutes or until firm to the touch at the edges and slightly puffed in appearance. Cool 1 minute on sheets. Transfer to wire racks with metal spatula and cool completely.

Variations:
Chocolate Covered Strawberry Thumbprints: Prepare as directed above but add ¾ cup miniature semisweet chocolate chips to the dough along with the egg yolks.

Pineapple Coconut Thumbprints: Prepare as directed above but use 1 teaspoon rum-flavored extract in place of the almond extract and add 2 teaspoons ground ginger to the dough. Roll dough balls in 1 cup flaked sweetened coconut, pressing to coat. Use pineapple preserves in place of the strawberry jam.

Lemon Heaven Thumbprints: Prepare as directed above but use lemon cake mix in place of white cake mix, 2 teaspoons grated lemon zest in place of almond extract, and jarred lemon curd in place of jam.

Chocolate Raspberry Thumbprints: Prepare as directed above but use chocolate cake mix in place of white cake mix and seedless raspberry preserves in place of jam.

Makes about 3½ dozen cookies.

Strawberry-Cream Cheese Thumbprints

Old-fashioned Blackberry Thumbprints

Wheat germ lends an extra-toasty, old-fashioned flavor to these tea-wonderful cookies. Be sure to use toasted wheat germ as opposed to raw wheat germ—the latter will impart an unpleasant flavor to the dough. Blackberry is a delicious flavor contrast to the rich dough, but you can substitute the jam, preserves, or jelly of your choice.

1	18.25-ounce package yellow cake mix
1	cup toasted wheat germ (e.g., Kretschmer's®)
¼	cup (½ stick) butter, softened
1	3-ounce package cream cheese, softened
2	large egg yolks
1	teaspoon vanilla extract
⅔	cup blackberry jam, stirred to loosen

Preheat oven to 350°. Position oven rack to upper third of the oven. Set aside two ungreased cookie sheets.

In a large bowl place the cake mix, wheat germ, softened butter, and cream cheese. Blend with an electric mixer set on low speed for 1–2 minutes, until mixture is blended and resembles fresh bread crumbs. Add the egg yolks and vanilla extract; beat on low speed 1–2 minutes longer, until dough comes together into a ball.

Shape dough into 1-inch balls. Position 2 inches apart on cookie sheets. Push an indentation into the center of each cookie with your thumb, the back of a rounded ¼-teaspoon measuring spoon, or cork. Fill each indentation with ¼ teaspoon jam.

Bake 8–10 minutes until firm to the touch at the edges and slightly puffed in appearance. Cool 1 minute on sheets. Transfer to wire racks with metal spatula and cool completely.

Variation:

Nutty Thumbprints: Prepare as directed above but roll dough balls in 1 cup finely chopped nuts (e.g., walnuts, pecans, almonds, or peanuts). Use any variety of jam, preserves, or jelly.

Makes about 3½ dozen cookies.

Gloreo Cookies

Think of a favorite sandwich cookie that rhymes with "gloreo" and you'll know what these yummy treats are all about. The cookies are softer than their store-bought cousins, making for a homey, old-fashioned cookie.

1	18.25-ounce package devil's food cake mix
2	large eggs
6	tablespoons cold water, divided
2	tablespoons vegetable oil
¼	cup unsweetened cocoa powder
1	packet unflavored gelatin
1	cup vegetable shortening
2	teaspoons vanilla extract
1	16-ounce package powdered sugar

Preheat oven to 350°. Position oven rack in upper third of the oven. Spray cookie sheets with nonstick cooking spray.

In a large bowl place the cake mix, eggs, 2 tablespoons water, and oil. Blend with an electric mixer set on low speed for 1–2 minutes until mixture is blended.

Place the cocoa powder in a small dish. Shape dough into marble-size balls; place 2 inches apart on greased cookie sheets. Dip bottom of drinking glass into cocoa powder; slightly flatten each ball.

Bake 7–8 minutes, until just set. Remove at once from cookie sheet to paper towels; immediately flatten each cookie with a smooth spatula. Cool completely.

Meanwhile, in a small cup soften gelatin in remaining 4 tablespoons cold water. Place in a heatproof cup in pan of hot water until gelatin is melted and transparent. Cool completely.

In a medium bowl beat the shortening with an electric mixer set on high speed until fluffy; add vanilla extract and powdered sugar a little at a time. Beat in gelatin mixture. Refrigerate 30 minutes.

Shape filling into 1-inch balls. Place between the two bottom sides of the cooled cookies and press gently until the filling has spread to edges of cookie.

Makes 4 dozen cookies.

Gloreo Cookies

Lollipop Cookies

Looking for a great birthday party activity for a group of little girls? Make several batches of these cookies, set out the icing, candies, and sprinkles, and you'll have a great party all wrapped up. For an even fancier, festive option, buy extra-long wooden sticks (found in craft stores), place the finished cookies in small vases, and tie with ribbon.

1   18.25-ounce package vanilla cake mix
⅓   cup vegetable oil
2   large eggs
24   wooden sticks with rounded ends
1   recipe Cookie Decorating Icing (see page 207)
Assorted decorating candies and nonpareils

Preheat oven to 375°. Position oven rack in middle of oven. Set aside an ungreased cookie sheet.

In a large bowl place the cake mix, oil, and eggs. Blend with an electric mixer set on low speed for 1–2 minutes, until mixture is blended and all dry ingredients are moistened.

Drop dough by heaping, rounded tablespoonfuls, 3 inches apart, onto cookie sheet. Insert wooden stick in edge of dough until tip is in center.

Bake 8–11 minutes or until puffed and almost no indentation remains when touched. Cool 1 minute on cookie sheet. Transfer to wire rack and cool completely. Frost and decorate as desired.

Makes 2 dozen cookie pops.

Pumpkin Whoopies with Cinnamon Fluff Filling

These fluff-filled, hand-held "pies" are festive fun for kids and adults alike. The flavors of pumpkin and cinnamon fit the bill for all sorts of fall festivities from Halloween to hay rides.

1	cup canned pumpkin purée
⅓	cup butter, plus ½ cup (1 stick), softened, divided
1	18.25-ounce package spice cake mix
2	large eggs
½	cup milk
1	8-ounce package cream cheese, softened
2	cups sifted powdered sugar
½	7-ounce jar marshmallow creme
1	teaspoon vanilla extract
1	teaspoon ground cinnamon

Preheat oven to 375°. Position oven rack in middle of oven. Line a cookie sheet with parchment paper or foil (grease foil, if using).

In a large mixing bowl beat pumpkin and ⅓ cup softened butter with an electric mixer on medium speed until smooth. Add cake mix, eggs, and milk; beat on low speed until combined, and then on medium speed for 1 minute. By the heaping table-spoonfuls, drop mounds of batter, 3 inches apart, onto cookie sheet; keep remaining batter chilled. Bake 15 minutes or until set and lightly browned around edges.

Carefully remove from parchment or foil; cool on wire rack. Repeat with remaining batter, lining cooled cookie sheets each time with new parchment or foil. If desired, place cookies in a covered storage container with waxed paper between layers to prevent sticking. Store cookies at room temperature for 24 hours.

In a medium bowl beat the remaining ½ cup (1 stick) butter and cream cheese with an electric mixer set on high until smooth. Add the sifted powdered sugar, marshmallow creme, vanilla extract, and cinnamon; beat until blended and smooth.

Spread about 2½ tablespoons filling on flat side of one cookie; top with a second cookie. Repeat. Serve immediately or cover and chill up to 2 hours.

Makes 15 whoopies.

Devil's Food Whoopies with Cocoa Fluff Filling

These showstoppers reward a little bit of work with a whole heap of praise. Kids can help with the final assembly of the whoopies— they'll love saying the name as much as eating their efforts.

1	cup jarred, unsweetened applesauce
⅓	cup butter, plus ½ cup (1 stick), softened, divided
1	18.25-ounce package devil's food cake mix
2	large eggs
½	cup milk
1	cup miniature semisweet chocolate chips, optional
1	8-ounce package cream cheese, softened
1⅔	cups powdered sugar, sifted
⅓	cup unsweetened cocoa powder, sifted
½	of a 7-ounce jar marshmallow creme
1	teaspoon vanilla extract

Preheat oven to 375°. Position oven rack in middle of oven. Line a cookie sheet with parchment paper or foil (grease foil, if using).

In a large mixing bowl beat applesauce and ⅓ cup softened butter with an electric mixer on medium speed until smooth. Add cake mix, eggs, and milk; beat on low speed until combined, and then on medium speed for 1 minute. Stir in miniature chocolate chips, if desired. By heaping tablespoonfuls, drop mounds of batter, 3 inches apart, onto cookie sheet; keep remaining batter chilled. Bake 15 minutes or until set and lightly browned around edges.

Carefully remove from parchment or foil; cool on wire rack. Repeat with remaining batter, lining cooled cookie sheets each time with new parchment or foil. If desired, place cookies in a covered storage container with waxed paper between layers to prevent sticking. Store cookies at room temperature for 24 hours.

In a medium bowl beat remaining ½ cup (1 stick) softened butter and softened cream cheese with an electric mixer set on high until smooth. Add the sifted powdered sugar, cocoa powder, marshmallow creme, and vanilla; beat until blended and smooth.

Spread about 2½ tablespoons filling on flat side of one cookie; top with a second cookie. Repeat. Serve immediately or cover and chill up to 2 hours.

Makes 15 whoopies.

Devil's Food Whoopies with Cocoa Fluff Filling

Peanut Butter Chocolate Kiss Thumbprints

This favorite recipe makes enough to feed a small army of cookie monsters. Although delicious when eaten right away, these cookies taste even better if you have the time to make them a day ahead.

1   18.25-ounce package yellow cake mix
1   14-ounce can sweetened condensed milk
1   cup chunky-style peanut butter
1   large egg
2   teaspoons vanilla extract
1   13-ounce package chocolate "kiss" candies, unwrapped

Preheat oven to 350°. Position oven rack in middle of oven. Set aside two ungreased cookie sheets.

In a large mixing bowl mix the cake mix, condensed milk, peanut butter, egg, and vanilla extract with an electric mixer set on low speed for 1–2 minutes, until all dry ingredients are moistened and dough is well blended (dough will be very thick).

Shape dough into 1-inch balls and position 2 inches apart on cookie sheets.

Bake 8–10 minutes, until firm to the touch at the edges and slightly puffed in appearance. Remove sheets from the oven and immediately push a kiss candy, flat side down, into the center of each cookie. Cool 1 minute on sheets. Transfer to wire racks with metal spatula and cool completely.

Variation:

Peanut Butter Caramel Thumbprints: Prepare as directed above but use chocolate-covered caramel candies (e.g., Rolos®) in place of the kiss candies.

Makes about 6 dozen cookies.

Peppery Pecan-Chocolate Crackles

*Take a walk on the spicy side with a kick of cayenne and a dash of
cinnamon in these easy chocolate cookies. If you like, add a slick of
Chocolate Ganache (page 207) to cool things down.*

1	18.25-ounce package devil's food cake mix
¼	cup unsweetened cocoa powder
⅛	teaspoon cayenne pepper
2	large eggs, lightly beaten
2	tablespoons butter, softened
2	tablespoons milk
1	cup finely chopped pecans

Preheat oven to 375°. Position oven rack in middle of oven. Set aside ungreased
cookie sheet.

In a large bowl place half of the cake mix along with the cocoa powder, cayenne
pepper, eggs, and softened butter. Blend with an electric mixer set on low speed for
1–2 minutes, until mixture is blended. Stir in remaining cake mix until all dry ingredients are blended (dough will be stiff).

Place milk in a shallow dish. Place pecans in another shallow dish. Roll dough into
1-inch balls. Dip balls in milk, then roll in nuts to coat. Place 2 inches apart on ungreased cookie sheet.

Bake 8–9 minutes or until tops appear cracked. Cool 1 minute on sheet. Transfer to
a wire rack and let cool completely.

Makes 2½ dozen cookies.

Vanilla Bliss Cookies

All you need to make and enjoy these cookies is a big sweet tooth and a fondness for vanilla.

1	18.25-ounce package vanilla cake mix
1	3.4-ounce package instant vanilla pudding mix
½	cup vegetable oil
1	egg
½	cup sour cream (not reduced fat)
2	teaspoons vanilla extract
⅔	cup quick-cooking oats
1½	cups vanilla baking chips or white chocolate chips

Preheat oven to 350°. Position oven rack in middle of oven. Spray cookie sheets with nonstick cooking spray.

In a large bowl place half of the cake mix along with the instant pudding mix, oil, egg, sour cream, and vanilla extract. Blend with an electric mixer set on low speed for 1–2 minutes until mixture is blended and smooth. Stir in oats and chips.

Shape dough into 1½ inch balls; place 2 inches apart on the prepared cookie sheets.

Bake 11–13 minutes until golden at edges and just barely set at center. Cool cookies on cookie sheet 5 minutes (cookies will continue to firm). Transfer to a wire rack; cool completely.

Variations:

Butterscotch Bliss Cookies: Prepare as directed above but use yellow cake mix, instant butterscotch pudding, and butterscotch baking chips.

Triple-Chocolate Bliss Cookies: Prepare as directed above but use chocolate cake mix, instant chocolate pudding, and semisweet chocolate chips.

Peanut Butter Bliss Cookies: Prepare as directed above but use yellow cake mix, instant butterscotch pudding, and peanut butter–flavored baking chips. Additionally, use ½ cup creamy peanut butter in place of the sour cream.

Makes about 4 dozen cookies.

Coconut Macaroons

*I'm a bit of a snob about macaroons—I like the kind that
strike a good balance between chewy and crisp with just a slight
nuance of almond flavor. This recipe fits the bill. Better still, you can
bang out a batch in well under an hour.*

1	18.25-ounce package white cake mix
1	cup water
⅓	cup vegetable oil
3	large egg whites
¾	teaspoon almond extract
2	14-ounce packages sweetened flaked coconut

Preheat oven to 350°. Position oven rack in middle of oven. Grease cookie sheets with vegetable shortening.

In a large bowl place the cake mix, water, oil, egg whites, and almond extract. Blend with an electric mixer set on medium speed 1–2 minutes; stop mixer and scrape down sides of bowl with rubber spatula. Blend 1 minute longer on medium-high speed until smooth and all dry ingredients are moistened. Stir in coconut with a wooden spoon until blended.

Drop dough by rounded tablespoonfuls onto prepared sheets.

Bake 12–14 minutes or until golden brown. Transfer cookies to wire rack with metal spatula and cool completely.

Variation:

Chocolate-Chip Macaroons: Prepare as directed above but add 2 cups miniature semisweet chocolate chips to the batter along with the coconut.

Makes about 6 dozen cookies.

Snow-capped Chocolate Crinkles

My friend Abby wanted to know who first hypothesized that combining frozen whipped topping and cake mix could lead to a great cookie. Good question. And while I don't have the answer, I do know that these easy cookies are loved by one and all and are a last-minute saving grace when a batch of cookies is needed in a pinch. They get their "snow-capped" appearance when the powdered sugar tops crack as they bake.

1	18.25-ounce package chocolate cake mix
2	large eggs
1¾	cups frozen whipped topping, thawed
1	cup powdered sugar, sifted

In a large bowl place the cake mix, eggs, and thawed whipped topping. Blend 1–2 minutes with an electric mixer set on medium speed until well blended and all dry ingredients are moistened (dough will be stiff). Refrigerate dough, covered, for 30 minutes.

Preheat oven to 350°. Position oven rack in middle of oven. Set aside ungreased cookie sheets. Place sifted powdered sugar in a small, shallow dish.

Shape dough into 1-inch balls. Roll cookies in powdered sugar to coat. Place 2 inches apart on ungreased cookie sheet.

Bake 10–12 minutes or until cookies are puffed in appearance and firm at edges (centers will still be slightly soft). Let cookies rest on cookie sheets 2 minutes (cookies will fall, giving them a cracked appearance).

Transfer cookies to wire rack with metal spatula and cool completely.

Makes about 5 dozen cookies.

Gingersnap Crinkles

Turbinado sugar (sometimes called "raw" sugar) adds a sophisti-
cated sparkle and crunch to these spicy favorites. If you cannot find
it, regular sugar works just fine as a substitute. Be sure to make
these in fall and serve with mugfuls of hot apple cider.

1   18.25-ounce package spice cake mix
2   large eggs
1¾   cups frozen whipped topping, thawed
1½   teaspoons ground ginger
½   teaspoon ground cinnamon
⅛   teaspoon ground black pepper
¾   cup turbinado sugar

In a large bowl place the cake mix, eggs, thawed whipped topping, ginger, cinnamon, and black pepper. Blend 1–2 minutes with an electric mixer set on medium speed until well blended and all dry ingredients are moistened (dough will be stiff). Refrigerate dough, covered, for 30 minutes.

Preheat oven to 350°. Position oven rack in middle of oven. Set aside ungreased cookie sheets. Place turbinado sugar into a small, shallow dish.

Shape dough into 1-inch balls. Roll cookies in sugar to coat. Place 2 inches apart on ungreased cookie sheet.

Bake 10–12 minutes or until cookies are puffed in appearance and firm at edges (centers will still be slightly soft). Let cookies rest on cookie sheets 2 minutes (cookies will fall, giving them a cracked appearance).

Transfer cookies to wire rack with metal spatula and cool completely.

Makes about 5 dozen cookies.

Butterscotch Crispy Cookies

Part crispy rice treat, part cookie, 100 percent yummy—these indispensable treats are ideal mates for tall, cold glasses of milk.

1	18.25-ounce package yellow cake mix
¼	cup packed dark brown sugar
1	cup (2 sticks) butter, softened
2	large eggs
2	tablespoons milk
1½	cups butterscotch baking chips
3	cups crisp rice cereal, divided

Preheat oven to 350°. Position oven rack in middle of oven. Spray cookie sheets with nonstick cooking spray.

In a large bowl place the cake mix, brown sugar, softened butter, eggs, and milk. Blend with an electric mixer set on low speed for 2 minutes, until well blended. Fold in butterscotch chips and 1½ cups cereal. Refrigerate 1 hour.

Coarsely crush remaining 1½ cups cereal into coarse crumbs; place in shallow dish.

Shape dough into 1-inch balls. Roll in crushed cereal. Place on prepared cookie sheets about 1 inch apart.

Bake 11–13 minutes or until set at edges and just barely set at center when lightly touched. Cool 1 minute on sheets. Transfer to wire racks with metal spatula and cool completely.

Variation:

Chocolate Crispy Cookies: Prepare as directed above but use chocolate cake mix in place of yellow cake mix and semisweet chocolate chips in place of butterscotch baking chips.

Makes about 4½ dozen cookies.

Maple Sugar Cookies

Maple has been a favorite American flavoring since Native Americans first taught the early colonists how to tap trees for their sap. Pure maple syrup is the best choice here, but for a less expensive option, substitute a maple-flavored pancake syrup.

1	18.25-ounce package yellow cake mix
¼	cup packed light brown sugar
¼	teaspoon baking soda
2	tablespoons butter, melted
1	large egg yolk
¼	cup pure maple syrup
2	teaspoons maple-flavored extract
⅔	cup turbinado (or "raw") sugar

In a large bowl place half of the cake mix along with the brown sugar, baking soda, melted butter, egg yolk, maple syrup, and maple extract. Blend 1–2 minutes with an electric mixer set on medium speed until well blended and all dry ingredients are moistened (dough will be stiff). Stir in remaining cake mix. Chill dough 1 hour.

Preheat oven to 375°. Position oven rack in middle of oven. Spray cookie sheets with nonstick cooking spray.

Place turbinado sugar in shallow dish. Roll dough into 1-inch balls. Roll each ball in sugar to coat. Place balls 2 inches apart on prepared cookie sheets. Flatten slightly.

Bake 9–10 minutes or until surface cracks and cookies are firm. Transfer to wire racks and cool completely.

Makes about 3 dozen cookies.

Chocolate-Vanilla Pinwheel Cookies

These pretty cookies may take a few more steps than other options in this book, but the results are well worth it. Get ready for the compliments!

½   **cup vegetable shortening**
⅓   **cup plus 1 tablespoon butter, softened, divided**
2   **large egg yolks**
1   **teaspoon vanilla extract**
1   **18.25-ounce package vanilla cake mix**
2½   **tablespoons unsweetened cocoa powder**

In a large bowl place the shortening, ⅓ cup softened butter, egg yolks, and vanilla extract. Blend with an electric mixer set on medium-high speed 1–2 minutes, until blended and smooth. Add cake mix to bowl; blend on low speed 1–2 minutes, until all dry ingredients are incorporated.

Divide dough in half. To one half of the dough, add remaining tablespoon butter and cocoa powder; knead until chocolate colored and thoroughly blended.

Place yellow dough between 2 pieces of waxed paper and roll into an 18 x 12 x ⅛-inch rectangle. Repeat with chocolate dough. Remove top piece of waxed paper from each piece of dough. Place one rectangle on top of the other and roll up like a jelly roll, beginning with long side. Tightly wrap in plastic wrap and refrigerate at least 2 hours.

Preheat oven to 350°. Position oven rack in middle of oven. Spray cookie sheets with nonstick cooking spray.

With a sharp knife slice dough into ⅛-inch-thick slices; place 1 inch apart on prepared cookie sheets. Bake 9–11 minutes. Cool 2 minutes on sheets. Transfer to wire racks with metal spatula and cool completely.

Makes about 3½ dozen cookies.

Molasses Spice Cookies

Here is a homespun cookie that tastes like gingerbread—
perfect for feeling cozy on cold days and nights.

1	18.25-ounce package spice cake mix
¾	teaspoon ground cinnamon
¾	teaspoon ground ginger
⅛	teaspoon ground cloves
¼	teaspoon baking soda
2	tablespoons vegetable oil
1	large egg yolk
¼	cup dark molasses
2	teaspoons vanilla extract
⅔	cup granulated sugar

In a large bowl place half of the cake mix along with the cinnamon, ginger, cloves, baking soda, oil, egg yolk, molasses, and vanilla extract. Blend with an electric mixer set on medium-high speed 1–2 minutes, until blended and smooth. Stir in remaining cake mix. Chill dough 1 hour.

Preheat oven to 375°. Position oven rack in middle of oven. Spray cookie sheets with nonstick cooking spray. Place sugar in shallow dish.

Roll dough into 1-inch balls; roll in sugar to coat. Place balls 2 inches apart on prepared cookie sheets. Flatten slightly with palm or bottom of a glass.

Bake 9–10 minutes or until surface cracks and cookies are firm. Transfer to wire racks and cool completely.

Makes about 3 dozen cookies.

Sesame Honey Crinkles

Culinary historians contend that sesame is one of the first recorded seasonings, dating back to 3000 B.C. In addition to a traditional role in Middle Eastern and Indian cuisines, sesame also has a rich culinary role in the cuisine of the American South. One bite of these cookies reveals that sesame is quintessentially suited to honey, making this recipe an all-American winner.

1   18.25-ounce package yellow cake mix
1   cup all-purpose flour
½   cup (1 stick) butter, melted
¼   cup honey
2   large eggs
¾   cup sesame seeds

Preheat oven to 375°. Position oven rack in middle of oven. Spray cookie sheets with nonstick cooking spray.

In a large bowl place half of the cake mix along with the flour, melted butter, honey, and eggs. Blend with electric mixer set on low speed 1 minute; stop mixer and scrape bowl. Beat on low speed 1–2 minutes longer, until well blended. Stir in remaining cake mix. Chill dough 1 hour.

Place sesame seeds in shallow dish. Roll dough into 1-inch balls. Roll each ball in sesame seeds to coat. Place balls 2 inches apart on prepared cookie sheets. Flatten slightly.

Bake 9–10 minutes or until cookies are golden at the edges and just barely set at center. Transfer to wire racks and cool completely.

Variation:
Honey & Lemon Crinkles: Prepare as directed above but use lemon cake mix in place of yellow cake mix and roll cookies in granulated sugar rather than sesame seeds.

Makes about 4 dozen cookies.

Mocha-Hazelnut Sandwich Cookies

An elegant, contemporary cookie with European flair thanks to the chocolate-hazelnut spread. Look for the spread in one of two places in the supermarket: in the international foods section or the aisle where peanut butter can be found.

2	teaspoons instant coffee or espresso powder
2	teaspoons vanilla extract
1	18.25-ounce package German chocolate cake mix
⅓	cup vegetable oil
2	large eggs
¾	cup chocolate-hazelnut spread (e.g., Nutella)

Preheat oven to 350°. Position oven rack in middle of oven. Spray cookie sheets with nonstick cooking spray.

In a large bowl dissolve the espresso powder in the vanilla extract. To the same bowl add half of the cake mix along with the oil and eggs. Blend with an electric mixer set on medium-high speed 1–2 minutes, until blended and smooth. Stir in remaining cake mix.

Drop dough by teaspoonfuls on prepared cookie sheets.

Bake 8–10 minutes or until set at edges and just barely set at center when lightly touched and cookies have a cracked appearance (cookies will be flat and round). Cool 1 minute on sheets. Transfer to wire racks with metal spatula and cool completely.

Spread bottom half of one cookie with a teaspoon of chocolate-hazelnut spread; sandwich with a second cookie. Repeat with remaining cookies.

Makes about 3 dozen sandwich cookies.

German Chocolate Thumbprint Cookies

These decadent mouthfuls are worth every calorie.

1   cup packed light brown sugar
1   cup canned evaporated milk
½   cup (1 stick) plus ⅓ cup butter, softened, divided
3   large egg yolks, lightly beaten with a fork
1   teaspoon vanilla extract
1½   cups sweetened flaked coconut
1½   cups chopped pecans
1   18.25-ounce package German chocolate cake mix

In a heavy-bottomed medium saucepan, combine brown sugar, evaporated milk, ½ cup softened butter, and egg yolks. Cook over medium heat for 10–13 minutes or until thickened and bubbly, whisking frequently. Stir in vanilla extract, coconut, and pecans. Remove from heat; cool completely. Reserve 1¼ cups topping mixture; set aside.

Preheat oven to 350°. Position oven rack in middle of oven. In a large mixing bowl combine cake mix, remaining ⅓ cup softened butter, and remaining coconut-pecan mixture. Stir by hand until all dry ingredients are thoroughly moistened.

Shape dough into 1-inch balls. Place 2 inches apart on ungreased cookie sheets. With thumb or back of a teaspoon measure, make an indentation in center of each ball and fill with mounded ½ teaspoonful of reserved coconut-pecan mixture.

Bake 10–13 minutes or until just barely set. Cool 2 minutes on sheets. Transfer cookies with spatula to wire racks and cool completely.

Makes about 4½ dozen thumbprints.

Pastel Mint Meltaways

For a classy little tea party, an occasion is required—pretty linens, some fresh flowers, and, of course, an assortment of delicious and delicate cakes and cookies. These pastel mint dainties hit the mark.

1   18.25-ounce package white cake mix
1   8-ounce package cream cheese, softened
¼   cup (½ stick) butter, softened
1   large egg
1   teaspoon peppermint extract
1½ cups coarsely chopped pastel mints

Preheat oven to 375°. Position oven rack in middle of oven. Spray cookie sheets with nonstick cooking spray.

In a large bowl place the half of the cake mix along with the softened cream cheese, butter, egg, and peppermint extract. Blend with an electric mixer set on medium speed 1–2 minutes, until well blended and smooth. Stir in remaining cake mix and pastel mints until blended.

Shape dough into 1-inch balls. Place balls 2 inches apart on prepared cookie sheets.

Bake 10–12 minutes or until set at edges and just barely set at center when lightly touched. Cool 3–4 minutes on sheets (cookies will firm as they cool). Transfer to wire racks with metal spatula and cool completely.

Makes about 4 dozen cookies.

Dulce de Leche Crisps

A favorite confection in Latin American countries, dulce de leche is made by slowly reducing fresh milk and sugar until the mixture thickens into a luscious caramel. Here the beloved treat finds new life as a charming cookie that bakes up much like a crisp brandy snap with a lacy, brown-sugary center.

1   cup packed dark brown sugar
1   cup canned evaporated milk
½   cup (1 stick) plus ⅓ cup butter, softened, divided
3   large egg yolks, lightly beaten with a fork
1   teaspoon vanilla extract
1⅓ cups toffee baking bits
2   cups chopped pecans, walnuts, or almonds
1   18.25-ounce package white cake mix

In a heavy-bottomed medium saucepan, combine brown sugar, evaporated milk, ½ cup softened butter, and egg yolks. Cook over medium heat for 10–13 minutes or until thickened and bubbly, whisking frequently. Stir in vanilla extract. Remove from heat; cool completely. Stir the toffee bits and nuts into cooled mixture. Reserve 1¼ cups toffee mixture. Set aside.

Preheat oven to 350°. Position oven rack in middle of oven. In a large mixing bowl combine cake mix, remaining ⅓ cup softened butter, and remaining toffee mixture. Stir by hand until all dry ingredients are thoroughly moistened.

Shape dough into 1-inch balls. Place 2 inches apart on ungreased cookie sheets. With thumb or back of a teaspoon measure, make an indentation in center of each ball and fill with mounded ½ teaspoonful of the reserved brown sugar mixture.

Bake 10–13 minutes or until just barely set. Cool 2 minutes on sheets. Transfer cookies with spatula to wire racks and cool completely.

Makes about 4½ dozen cookies.

Caramel Pecan Turtle Cookies

Turtles are caramel and pecan candy clusters that are then covered in a thick swath of milk chocolate. To caramel lovers, like myself, they are heaven. Here's a quick and easy cookie version of the irresistible treat. Warning: do not leave yourself alone with a fresh batch.

1   18.25-ounce package chocolate cake mix
¼   cup (½ stick) butter, softened
2   large eggs
2   cups whole pecan halves
24   milk caramels, unwrapped
3   tablespoons milk

In a large bowl place half of the cake mix along with the softened butter and eggs. Blend with electric mixer on low speed 1 minute; stop mixer and scrape down bowl. Blend on low speed 1 minute longer. Stir in remaining cake mix. Cover bowl with plastic wrap and refrigerate dough at least 1 hour.

Preheat oven to 350°. Position oven rack in middle of oven. Spray cookie sheets with nonstick cooking spray.

Shape dough into 1-inch balls. Place 2 inches apart on prepared cookie sheets. Press one whole pecan half in center of each cookie.

Bake 9–11 minutes or until firm to the touch at the edges. Cool 1 minute on sheets. Transfer to wire racks with metal spatula and cool completely.

In a small saucepan set over low heat melt the caramels with the milk, stirring until melted and smooth; remove from heat. Drizzle caramel across cooled cookies using spoon or fork.

Makes about 4½ dozen cookies.

Snickerdoodles

Snickerdoodles, favorite American cookies dating back to nineteenth-century New England, are likely beloved for their whimsical name as much as their old-fashioned good taste. Whatever the case, these cinnamon-spiked, crisp-soft cookies have never been easier to prepare than with a package of cake mix.

1	18.25-ounce package white cake mix
¼	cup vegetable oil
2	large eggs, lightly beaten
½	teaspoon ground nutmeg
¼	cup sugar
2	teaspoons ground cinnamon

Preheat oven to 350°. Position oven rack in middle of oven. Spray cookie sheets with nonstick cooking spray.

In a large bowl place the cake mix, oil, eggs and nutmeg. Mix with a wooden spoon until just blended and all dry ingredients are moistened (dough will be stiff).

Combine the sugar and cinnamon in a shallow dish or bowl. Form dough into 1-inch balls; roll in cinnamon sugar. Place 2 inches apart on prepared cookie sheets.

Bake 10–12 minutes, until set at edges and just barely set at center when lightly touched. Cool 1 minute on sheets. Transfer to wire racks with metal spatula and cool completely.

Makes about 4 dozen cookies.

Classic Madeleines

French writer Marcel Proust praised the tender, buttery sponge cakes known as madeleines in his work Remembrance of Things Past. *You, too, will sing their praises once this recipe is tried. A few standard pantry items transform a box of yellow cake mix into these classic cookies, worthy of a Parisian patisserie.*

	Vegetable shortening and all-purpose flour to grease pans
1	18.25-ounce package yellow cake mix
½	cup (1 stick) butter, melted
¼	cup milk
4	large eggs, separated
2–3	tablespoons powdered sugar

Preheat oven to 350°. Position oven rack in middle of oven. Grease molds of large madeleine pan (about 3 x 1¼-inch shell molds) with vegetable shortening. Sprinkle with flour to coat pan, shaking off excess.

In a large bowl place the cake mix, melted butter, milk, and egg yolks. Blend 1–2 minutes with an electric mixer set on medium speed until well blended and smooth. Set aside momentarily. Clean beaters.

In another large mixing bowl beat the egg whites with electric mixer set on high speed until soft peaks form. Stir ¼ of the beaten egg whites into the cake batter to lighten it; fold remaining whites into batter.

Spoon 1 heaping tablespoon batter into each indentation in pan (do not overfill; batter will spread as it bakes). Bake until puffed and set at center, about 8–10 minutes. Cool in pan 5 minutes; gently remove madeleines to wire rack. Repeat process, greasing and flouring pan before each batch. Sift powdered sugar over cooled cookies.

Variation:

Almond Madeleines: Prepare as directed above but use vanilla cake mix in place of the yellow cake mix and add ¾ teaspoon almond extract to the batter.

Makes about 2½ dozen madeleines.

Mint Chocolate-Chip Madeleines

Peppermint gives these tender, chocolate-dotted madeleines a cool accent of refreshing flavor. Be sure to use miniature chocolate chips in the recipe—regular size chips will sink in the batter.

Vegetable shortening and all-purpose flour to grease pans
1 **18.25-ounce package vanilla cake mix**
½ **cup (1 stick) butter, melted**
¼ **cup milk**
4 **large eggs, separated**
1 **teaspoon peppermint extract**
1 **cup miniature semisweet chocolate chips**
2–3 **tablespoons powdered sugar**

Preheat oven to 350°. Position oven rack in middle of oven. Grease molds of large madeleine pan (about 3 x 1¼-inch shell molds) with vegetable shortening. Sprinkle with flour to coat pan, shaking off excess.

In a large bowl place the cake mix, melted butter, milk, egg yolks and peppermint extract. Blend 1–2 minutes with an electric mixer set on medium speed until well blended and smooth; stir in miniature chocolate chips. Set aside momentarily. Clean beaters.

In a large mixing bowl beat the egg whites with electric mixer set on high speed until soft peaks form. Stir one-fourth of the beaten egg whites into the cake batter to lighten it; fold remaining whites into batter.

Spoon 1 heaping tablespoonful of batter into each indentation in pan (do not overfill; batter will spread as it bakes). Bake until puffed and set at center, about 8–10 minutes. Cool in pan 5 minutes; gently remove madeleines to wire rack. Repeat process, greasing and flouring pan before each batch. Sift powdered sugar over cooled cookies.

Variations:

Double Chocolate Mint Madeleines: Prepare as directed above but use chocolate cake mix in place of the vanilla cake mix.

Mocha Chip Madeleines: Prepare as directed above but use chocolate cake mix in place of the vanilla cake mix. Eliminate the peppermint extract and in its place use 2½ teaspoons instant espresso or coffee powder that has been dissolved in 1½ teaspoons vanilla extract.

Makes about 3 dozen madeleines.

Mint Chocolate-Chip Madeleines

Florida Citrus Madeleines

I love these madeleines for their lightness and intense citrus flavor. The most difficult thing about making them is remembering to take it easy when folding the egg whites into the batter—the gentler the folding, the airier the madeleines. For a fancier final flourish, consider dipping each madeleine in melted white chocolate instead of dusting with powdered sugar.

Vegetable shortening and all-purpose flour to grease pans
1   18.25-ounce package lemon cake mix
½   cup (1 stick) butter, melted
¼   cup orange juice
1   tablespoon grated orange zest
4   large eggs, separated
2–3 tablespoons powdered sugar

Preheat oven to 350°. Position oven rack in middle of oven. Grease molds of large madeleine pan (about 3 x 1¼-inch shell molds) with vegetable shortening. Sprinkle with flour to coat pan, shaking off excess.

Place the cake mix, melted butter, orange juice, orange zest, and egg yolks in a large bowl. Blend with an electric mixer set on medium speed 1–2 minutes, until well blended and smooth. Set aside momentarily. Clean beaters.

In a large mixing bowl beat egg whites with electric mixer set on high speed until soft peaks form. Stir ¼ of the beaten egg whites into the cake batter to lighten it; fold remaining whites into batter.

Spoon 1 heaping tablespoon batter into each indentation in pan (do not overfill; batter will spread as it bakes). Bake until puffed and set at center, about 8–10 minutes. Cool in pan 5 minutes; gently remove madeleines to wire rack. Repeat process, greasing and flouring pan before each batch. Sift powdered sugar over cooled cookies.

Variations:

Orange Madeleines: Prepare as directed above but use orange cake mix in place of the lemon cake mix and, if desired, add ½ teaspoon ground coriander or cardamom to the batter.

Lemon Madeleines: Prepare as directed above but replace the orange juice with 2 tablespoons water and 2 tablespoons fresh lemon juice and use grated lemon zest in place of the orange zest. If desired, drizzle madeleines with Lemon Icing (see page 213).

Lemon-Lime Madeleines: Prepare as directed above but replace the orange juice with 2 tablespoons water and 2 tablespoons fresh lime juice and use grated lime zest in place of the orange zest. If desired, drizzle madeleines with Lime Icing (see page 213).

Makes about 2½ dozen madeleines.

Florida Citrus Madeleines

Chunky Chocolate Walnut Biscotti

A cup of espresso. An inspiring view. And one of these very chocolate biscotti. These cookies can make a coffee break a quick escape.

1	18.25-ounce package chocolate cake mix
1	cup all-purpose flour
½	cup (1 stick) butter, melted and cooled
2	large eggs
1⅓	cups semisweet chocolate chunks
1	cup coarsely chopped walnuts

Preheat oven to 350°. Position rack in center of oven. Spray cookie sheet with non-stick cooking spray.

In a large mixing bowl place cake mix, flour, melted butter, eggs, chocolate chunks, and walnuts. Blend with an electric mixer set on low speed until well-blended, about 2–3 minutes, scraping down sides of bowl (dough will be very stiff).

Transfer dough to prepared cookie sheet. With floured hands, shape dough into two rectangles, each 14 inches long by 3 inches wide, ¾-inch thick, spacing about 4–5 inches apart on sheet. Mound the dough so it is slightly higher in the middle than at the edges.

Bake 30–35 minutes until firm to touch; remove from oven and cool on sheet for ten minutes, leaving oven on.

Cutting on the cookie sheet, use a sharp kitchen knife to slice each rectangle into ¾-inch slices on the diagonal. Carefully turn these slices onto their sides.

Return cookie sheet to oven. Bake biscotti 10 minutes. Turn oven off and let biscotti remain in oven until crisp, about 30–40 minutes longer. Remove from oven and transfer biscotti to a rack. Cool completely.

Makes about 32 biscotti.

Pistachio-Lemon Biscotti

Cultivated in Mediterranean climates, pale green pistachios have a delicate flavor that pairs perfectly with lemon. Either raw or roasted unsalted pistachios can be used here with equally successful results.

1	**18.25-ounce package vanilla cake mix**
1	**cup all-purpose flour**
1	**tablespoon grated lemon zest**
½	**cup (1 stick) butter, melted and cooled**
2	**large eggs**
1⅓	**cups shelled natural pistachios**
1	**recipe Lemon Icing (see page 213)**

Preheat oven to 350°. Position rack in center of oven. Spray cookie sheet with non-stick cooking spray.

In a large mixing bowl place the cake mix, flour, lemon zest, melted butter, eggs and pistachios. Blend with an electric mixer set on low speed until well-blended, about 2–3 minutes, scraping down sides of bowl (dough will be very stiff).

Transfer dough to prepared cookie sheet. With floured hands, shape dough into two rectangles, each 14 inches long by 3 inches wide, ¾-inch thick, spacing about 4–5 inches apart on sheet. Mound the dough so it is slightly higher in the middle than at the edges.

Bake 30–35 minutes, until firm to touch; remove from oven (leave oven on) and cool on sheet for 10 minutes.

Cutting on the cookie sheet, use a sharp kitchen knife to slice each rectangle into ¾-inch slices on the diagonal. Carefully turn these slices onto their sides.

Return cookie sheet to oven. Bake biscotti 10 minutes. Turn oven off and let biscotti remain in oven until crisp, about 30–40 minutes longer. Remove from oven and transfer biscotti to a rack. Cool completely.

Prepare Lemon Icing and with a butter knife or small offset spatula spread over one side of each biscotti. Place on waxed paper–lined cookie sheet and refrigerate at least 30 minutes to set the icing. Store in an airtight container or ziplock bag for 2–3 weeks.

Makes about 32 biscotti.

Orange Poppyseed Biscotti

Poppyseeds—perhaps due to their polka-dotting potential—have a natural charm that always appeals. Here they grace a simple, orange-scented biscotti that comes together with ease. Like all biscotti, they are good candidates for a picnic since they travel well, and deliciously.

1   18.25-ounce package yellow cake mix
1   cup all-purpose flour
¼   cup poppyseeds
1½   tablespoons grated orange zest
½   cup (1 stick) butter, melted and cooled
2   large eggs
1   recipe Orange Icing (see page 213), optional

Preheat oven to 350°. Position rack in center of oven. Spray cookie sheet with non-stick cooking spray.

In a large mixing bowl place cake mix, flour, poppyseeds, orange zest, melted butter and eggs. Blend with an electric mixer set on low speed until well-blended, about 2–3 minutes, scraping down sides of bowl (dough will be very stiff).

Transfer dough to prepared cookie sheet. With floured hands, shape dough into two rectangles, each 14 inches long by 3 inches wide, ¾-inch thick, spacing about 4–5 inches apart on sheet. Mound the dough so it is slightly higher in the middle than at the edges.

Bake 30–35 minutes, until firm to touch; remove from oven (leave oven on) and cool on sheet for 10 minutes.

Cutting on the cookie sheet, use a sharp kitchen knife to slice each rectangle into (approximately) ¾-inch slices on the diagonal. Carefully turn these slices onto their sides.

Return cookie sheet to oven. Bake biscotti 10 minutes. Turn oven off and let biscotti remain in oven until crisp, about 30–40 minutes longer. Remove from oven and transfer biscotti to a rack. Cool completely. If desired, prepare Orange Icing and with a butter knife or small offset spatula spread over one side of each biscotti. Place on waxed paper–lined cookie sheet and refrigerate at least 30 minutes to set the icing. Store in an airtight container or plastic ziplock bag for 2–3 weeks.

Variation:

Lemon Poppyseed Biscotti: Prepare as directed above but substitute lemon zest for the orange zest and Lemon Icing (see page 213) for the Orange Icing.

Makes about 32 biscotti.

Apricot-Almond Biscotti

Despite a reputation as a temperamental treat, biscotti is simply a few basic ingredients blended into a dough and backed twice to create an impressive cookie perfect for dunking or nibbling along with a favorite hot drink. These particular biscotti, accented with bits of dried apricot and almond in each bite, are made all the easier thanks to cake mix. And they aren't as time-consuming as you might think. Surprisingly, you can make and bake an entire batch in under an hour.

1	18.25-ounce package vanilla cake mix
1	cup all-purpose flour
1	teaspoon almond extract
½	cup (1 stick) butter, melted and cooled
2	large eggs
1	cup chopped dried apricots
1	cup coarsely chopped almonds

Preheat oven to 350°. Position rack in center of oven. Spray cookie sheet with non-stick cooking spray.

In a large mixing bowl place the cake mix, flour, almond extract, melted butter, eggs, apricots, and almonds. Blend with an electric mixer set on low speed until well-blended, about 2–3 minutes, scraping down sides of bowl (dough will be very stiff).

Transfer dough to prepared cookie sheet. With floured hands, shape dough into two rectangles, each 14 inches long by 3 inches wide, ¾-inch thick, spacing about 4–5 inches apart on sheet. Mound the dough so it is slightly higher in the middle than at the edges.

Bake 30–35 minutes, until firm to touch; remove from oven (leave oven on) and cool on sheet for 10 minutes.

Cutting on the cookie sheet, use a sharp kitchen knife to slice each rectangle into ¾-inch slices on the diagonal. Carefully turn these slices onto their sides.

Return cookie sheet to oven. Bake biscotti 10 minutes. Turn oven off and let biscotti remain in oven until crisp, about 30–40 minutes longer. Remove from oven and transfer biscotti to a rack. Cool completely.

Variation:

Raisin & Cinnamon Biscotti: Prepare as directed above but substitute raisins for the apricots, chopped pecans for the almonds, vanilla extract for the almond extract, and add 2 teaspoons ground cinnamon to the dough.

Makes about 32 biscotti.

Café Brulot Biscotti

Café Brulot is a traditional New Orleans coffee drink, often served flaming, flavored with spices, orange peel, lemon peel, and brandy. Here it is in crunchy biscotti form.

2½	teaspoons instant espresso or coffee powder
2	teaspoons vanilla extract
1	18.25-ounce package vanilla cake mix
1	cup all-purpose flour
1	tablespoon grated lemon zest
1	tablespoon grated orange zest
½	cup (1 stick) butter, melted and cooled
2	large eggs
½	teaspoon ground cinnamon
¼	teaspoon ground cloves
1	recipe Brandy Icing (see page 217)

Preheat oven to 350°. Position rack in center of oven. Spray cookie sheet with non-stick cooking spray.

In a large bowl dissolve the espresso powder in the vanilla extract. Add the cake mix, flour, lemon zest, orange zest, melted butter, eggs, cinnamon, and cloves. Blend with an electric mixer set on low speed until well-blended, about 2–3 minutes, scraping down sides of bowl (dough will be very stiff).

Transfer dough to prepared cookie sheet. With floured hands, shape dough into two rectangles, each 14 inches long by 3 inches wide, ¾-inch thick, spacing about 4–5 inches apart on sheet. Mound the dough so it is slightly higher in the middle than at the edges.

Bake 30–35 minutes, until firm to touch; remove from oven (leave oven on) and cool on sheet for 10 minutes.

Cutting on the cookie sheet, use a sharp kitchen knife to slice each rectangle into ¾-inch slices on the diagonal. Carefully turn these slices onto their sides.

Return cookie sheet to oven. Bake biscotti 10 minutes. Turn oven off and let biscotti remain in oven until crisp, about 30–40 minutes longer. Remove from oven and transfer biscotti to a rack. Cool completely.

Prepare Brandy Icing and with a butter knife or small offset spatula spread over one side of each biscotti. Place on waxed paper–lined cookie sheet and refrigerate at least 30 minutes to set the icing. Store in an airtight container or plastic ziplock bag for 2–3 weeks.

Makes about 32 biscotti.

Nutty Coffee-Toffee Biscotti

These nut-studded biscotti, enriched further with both coffee and toffee, stand strong on their own but are also quite fine alongside your favorite coffee or espresso drink.

1	18.25-ounce package vanilla cake mix
1	cup all-purpose flour
1	tablespoon instant coffee or espresso powder
½	cup (1 stick) butter, melted and cooled
2	large eggs
½	teaspoon almond extract
1	cup English toffee baking bits
1½	cups very coarsely chopped almonds

Preheat oven to 350°. Position rack in center of oven. Spray cookie sheet with non-stick cooking spray.

In a large mixing bowl place the cake mix, flour, coffee powder, melted butter, eggs, almond extract, toffee bits, and almonds. Blend with an electric mixer set on low speed until well-blended, about 2–3 minutes, scraping down sides of bowl (dough will be very stiff).

Transfer dough to prepared cookie sheet. With floured hands, shape dough into two rectangles, each 14 inches long by 3 inches wide, ¾-inch thick, spacing about 4–5 inches apart on sheet. Mound the dough so it is slightly higher in the middle than at the edges.

Bake 30–35 minutes or until firm to touch; remove from oven (leave oven on) and cool on sheet for 10 minutes.

Cutting on the cookie sheet, use a sharp kitchen knife to slice each rectangle into ¾-inch slices on the diagonal. Carefully turn these slices onto their sides.

Return cookie sheet to oven. Bake biscotti 10 minutes. Turn oven off and let biscotti remain in oven until crisp, about 30–40 minutes longer. Remove from oven and transfer biscotti to a rack. Cool completely.

Makes about 32 biscotti.

White Chocolate–Cranberry Biscotti

This biscotti is as beautiful as it is delicious and makes an especially appealing gift. You can transform this recipe into a dark chocolate treat by substituting chocolate cake mix for the vanilla cake mix and semisweet chocolate-chips for the white chocolate chips.

1	18.25-ounce package vanilla cake mix
1	cup all-purpose flour
½	cup (1 stick) butter, melted and cooled
2	large eggs
1	teaspoon almond extract
1	cup dried cranberries
1	cup white chocolate chips

Preheat oven to 350°. Position rack in center of oven. Spray cookie sheet with non-stick cooking spray.

In a large mixing bowl place the cake mix, flour, melted butter, eggs, almond extract, cranberries, and white chocolate chips. Blend with an electric mixer set on low speed until well-blended, about 2–3 minutes, scraping down sides of bowl (dough will be very stiff).

Transfer dough to prepared cookie sheet. With floured hands, shape dough into two rectangles, each 14 inches long by 3 inches wide, ¾-inch thick, spacing about 4–5 inches apart on sheet. Mound the dough so it is slightly higher in the middle than at the edges.

Bake 30–35 minutes until firm to touch; remove from oven (leave oven on) and cool on sheet for 10 minutes.

Cutting on the cookie sheet, use a sharp kitchen knife to slice each rectangle into ¾-inch slices on the diagonal. Carefully turn these slices onto their sides.

Return cookie sheet to oven. Bake biscotti 10 minutes. Turn oven off and let biscotti remain in oven until crisp, about 30–40 minutes longer. Remove from oven and transfer biscotti to a rack. Cool completely. Store in an airtight container or plastic ziplock bag for 2–3 weeks.

Makes about 32 biscotti.

Ginger Lover's Biscotti

One of my favorite family rituals is afternoon tea. We stop what we're doing, plug in the kettle and load up a tray with an assortment of nibbles. This biscotti is a favorite with my ginger-loving parents and siblings. Don't be put off by the addition of black pepper to the dough— it enhances the peppery bite of the ginger.

1	18.25-ounce package vanilla cake mix
1	cup all-purpose flour
2½	teaspoons ground ginger
¼	teaspoon finely ground black pepper
½	cup (1 stick) butter, melted and cooled
2	teaspoons vanilla extract
2	large eggs
⅔	cup finely chopped crystallized ginger

Preheat oven to 350°. Position rack in center of oven. Spray cookie sheet with non-stick cooking spray.

In a large mixing bowl place the cake mix, flour, ground ginger, ground pepper, melted butter, vanilla extract, eggs, and crystallized ginger. Blend with an electric mixer set on low speed until well-blended, about 2–3 minutes, scraping down sides of bowl.

Transfer dough to prepared cookie sheet. With floured hands, shape dough into two rectangles, each 14 inches long by 3 inches wide, ¾-inch thick, spacing about 4–5 inches apart on sheet. Mound the dough so it is slightly higher in the middle than at the edges.

Bake 30–35 minutes, until firm to touch; remove from oven (leave oven on) and cool on sheet for 10 minutes.

Cutting on the cookie sheet, use a sharp kitchen knife to slice each rectangle into ¾-inch slices on the diagonal. Carefully turn these slices onto their sides.

Return cookie sheet to oven. Bake biscotti 10 minutes. Turn oven off and let biscotti remain in oven until crisp, about 30–40 minutes longer. Remove from oven and transfer biscotti to a rack. Cool completely. Store in an airtight container or plastic ziplock bag for 2–3 weeks.

Makes about 32 biscotti.

Bahamas Biscotti

The flavors of the Caribbean—toasted coconut, ginger, and lime—enrich this simple biscotti dough for a unique crispy-crunchy cookie.

1   18.25-ounce package white cake mix
2   teaspoons ground ginger
1   tablespoon oil
2   large eggs
1   cup sweetened flaked coconut, lightly toasted
½   cup slivered almonds, lightly toasted
1   tablespoon grated lime zest
1   recipe Lime Icing (see page 213) or 1 recipe White Chocolate Dip (see page 206), optional

Preheat oven to 350°. Position rack in center of oven. Set aside an ungreased cookie sheet.

In a large bowl stir together the cake mix, ginger, oil, and eggs with a wooden spoon until blended and all dry ingredients are incorporated. Stir in the coconut, almonds, and lime zest by hand (dough will be stiff).

On the ungreased cookie sheet shape dough into a 15-inch-long, 4-inch-wide rectangle.

Bake 22–25 minutes, until golden and just set at the center when touched. On cookie sheet, cut log crosswise into ½-inch-thick slices; turn slices onto their sides.

Bake 10 minutes longer. Remove from oven and let cool on sheets 5 minutes. Transfer biscotti to a wire rack with a metal spatula and cool completely. If desired, prepare Lime Icing or White Chocolate Dip; drizzle over cooled biscotti. Place on waxed paper–lined cookie sheet and refrigerate at least 1 hour to set icing or chocolate. Store in an airtight container or plastic ziplock bag for 1–2 weeks.

Makes about 30 biscotti.

Buttery Cutout Cookies

You can't please all of the people all of the time—unless, that is, you're a warm butter cookie, fresh from the oven.

1	18.25-ounce package vanilla cake mix
¾	cup (1½ sticks) butter, softened
1	large egg
1	teaspoon vanilla extract
1	recipe Cookie Decorating Icing (see page 207)

In a large bowl place the cake mix, butter, egg and vanilla extract. Blend with an electric mixer set on low speed for 2 minutes, until blended and mixture comes together as a dough (dough will be very thick). Scrape the dough off of the beaters and wrap the bowl in plastic wrap. Chill, covered, at least 4 hours or overnight.

Preheat oven to 350°. Position racks to upper and lower positions of oven. Sprinkle a work surface with a thin layer of flour. Set out rolling pin, cookie cutters, metal spatula, two cookie sheets, and cooling racks.

Remove the dough from the refrigerator and divide into fourths. Place one-fourth of the dough on floured surface (cover and return remaining dough to refrigerator). Flour the rolling pin and roll dough to ¼-inch thickness. Flour cookie cutters and cut out shapes. Transfer dough to ungreased cookie sheets with spatula. Reroll any scraps, then repeat with remaining dough, rolling one-fourth at a time.

Place one sheet on each oven rack. Bake 4 minutes. Rotate the sheets (place the sheet from the bottom rack on the top rack and the sheet from the top rack on the bottom rack; this ensures even baking). Bake 2–3 minutes longer for small shapes, 5–7 minutes for large shapes, or until center is puffed and sinks back.

Remove from oven and let cookies rest on sheets 1 minute. Transfer with metal spatula to racks and cool completely. Prepare cookie decorating icing, or other icing of choice. Decorate cookies with icing.

Variation:

Buttery Chocolate Cutouts: Prepare as directed above but use chocolate cake mix in place of the vanilla cake mix.

Makes about 5 dozen 2½-inch cookies.

Coriander Lemon Cookies

Coriander leaves (cilantro) are well known and much used in contemporary kitchens, but the delicious seeds, though readily available, are far less familiar. The ground seeds have a mild fragrance, which some describe as a combination of lemon, sage, and cardamom. The spice is an exquisite enhancement in delicate baked goods such as these elegant slice-and-bake lemon cookies. The dough may also be rolled out and cut out with decorative cookie cutters.

1	18.25-ounce package lemon cake mix
½	cup vegetable shortening
⅓	cup butter, softened
1	large egg
1	tablespoon grated lemon zest
½	teaspoon ground coriander or ¼ teaspoon ground nutmeg

3–4 tablespoons powdered sugar or 1 recipe Lemon Icing (see page 213), optional

In a large bowl place the cake mix, shortening, softened butter, egg, lemon zest, and ground coriander. Blend with an electric mixer set on low speed for 1 minute until blended (dough will be very thick). Scrape the dough off of the beaters. Divide dough in half; shape each half into a 12 x 2-inch roll. Wrap each roll in plastic food wrap; refrigerate until firm (at least 4 hours).

Preheat oven to 350°. Position rack in center of oven. Cut rolls into ¼-inch slices with a sharp kitchen knife. Place 2 inches apart on ungreased cookie sheets.

Bake 7–8 minutes or until edges are lightly browned. Let stand on cookie sheets 1 minute. Transfer to wire rack and cool completely. Sprinkle with powdered sugar or ice with Lemon Icing, if desired.

Makes about 5 dozen cookies.

Gingerbread People

An afternoon spent making, baking, and decorating these nostalgic cut-out cookies is perfect for preheating memories, folding in both friends and family, and baking up good times.

1	18.25-ounce package spice cake mix
¾	cup all-purpose flour
2½	teaspoons ground ginger
1	teaspoon ground cinnamon
2	large eggs
⅓	cup vegetable oil
⅓	cup molasses
1	recipe Vanilla Icing (see page 216)
	Red Hots cinnamon candies or raisins, optional

In a large bowl place the cake mix, flour, ginger, and cinnamon; stir to combine. Add the eggs, oil, and molasses. Mix with a wooden spoon until well blended and all dry ingredients are moistened. Chill, covered, at least 4 hours or up to overnight.

Preheat oven to 375° and spray cookie sheets with nonstick cooking spray. Position racks to upper and lower positions of oven.

Sprinkle a work surface with a thin layer of flour. Set out rolling pin, 4-inch gingerbread person cookie cutters, metal spatula, and cooling racks.

Remove the dough from the refrigerator and divide into fourths. Place one-fourth of the dough on floured surface (cover and return remaining dough to refrigerator). Flour the rolling pin and roll dough to ¼-inch thickness. Flour cookie cutters and cut out shapes. Transfer dough to prepared cookie sheets with spatula. Re-roll any scraps, then repeat with remaining dough, rolling one fourth at a time.

Place one sheet on each oven rack. Bake 4 minutes. Rotate the sheets (place the sheet from the bottom rack on the top rack and the sheet from the top rack on the bottom rack. This ensures even baking). Bake 4–7 minutes for large shapes or until center is puffed and sinks back.

Remove from oven and let cookies rest on sheets 1 minute. Transfer with metal spatula to racks and cool completely. Prepare Vanilla Icing, or other icing of choice. Decorate cookies with icing and candies or raisins, if desired.

Makes about 2 dozen 4-inch cookies.

Cinnamon Slices

*When these cookie are baking in the oven, it's easy
to understand why the ancient Romans used cinnamon
as a perfume—the scent is decidedly aphrodisiacal.*

1   **18.25-ounce package spice cake mix**
½   **cup shortening**
⅓   **cup butter, softened**
1   **large egg**
2   **teaspoons ground cinnamon**
1½   **cups raw sugar, optional**

Place the cake mix, shortening, softened butter, egg and cinnamon in a large bowl. Blend with an electric mixer set on low speed for 1 minute (dough will be very thick). Scrape the dough off of the beaters. Divide dough in half; shape each half into 12x2-inch roll.

If desired, place raw sugar on a shallow plate; roll each log in the sugar, pressing gently to adhere. Wrap each roll in plastic food wrap; refrigerate until firm (at least 3 hours).

Preheat oven to 350°. Position rack in center of oven. Cut rolls into ¼-inch slices with a sharp kitchen knife. Place 2 inches apart on ungreased cookie sheets.

Bake 7–8 minutes or until edges are lightly browned. Let stand on cookie sheets 1 minute. Transfer to wire rack and cool completely.

Variation:
Caramel-Spice Sandwich Cookies: Prepare cookies as directed above. Prepare 1 recipe of Quick Caramel Frosting (see page 211); sandwich a tablespoon of frosting between two cookies. Repeat with remaining cookies and frosting.

Makes about 5 dozen cookies.

Slice-and-Bake
Toasted Coconut Cookies

No need to pre-toast the coconut here—because the cookies
are sliced thin, the coconut toasts in the dough as it bakes.
Delicious plain, these cookies are also heavenly drizzled
with Citrus Icing (see page 213).

1	**18.25-ounce package white cake mix**
½	**cup vegetable shortening**
⅓	**cup butter, softened**
1	**large egg**
1½	**teaspoons rum-flavored extract, optional**
1½	**cups sweetened flaked coconut**

In a large bowl place the cake mix, shortening, butter, egg, and rum extract, if desired. Blend with an electric mixer set on low speed for 1 minute or until blended (dough will be very thick). Scrape the dough off of the beaters. Stir in the coconut by hand.

Divide dough in half; shape each half into a 12 x 2-inch roll. Wrap each roll in plastic food wrap; refrigerate until firm (at least 4 hours).

Preheat oven to 350°. Position rack in center of oven. Cut rolls into ¼-inch slices with a sharp kitchen knife. Place 2 inches apart on ungreased cookie sheets.

Bake 7–8 minutes or until edges are lightly browned. Let stand on cookie sheets 1 minute. Transfer to wire rack and cool completely.

Variation:
Coconut Chocolate Ganache Sandwich Cookies: Prepare cookies as directed above. Prepare 1 recipe of Chocolate Ganache (see page 207); sandwich a tablespoon of ganache between two cookies. Repeat with remaining cookies and ganache.

Makes about 5 dozen cookies.

Orange & Honey Cutouts

Choose a light flavored honey, such as orange blossom or clover honey, in these delicately flavored cut-out cookies for optimal results.

1   **18.25-ounce package orange or yellow cake mix**
¾   **cup all-purpose flour**
2   **large eggs**
⅓   **cup butter, melted**
⅓   **cup honey**
1   **tablespoon grated orange zest**
1   **recipe Orange Icing (see page 213)**
2–3 **tablespoons orange-colored decorating sugar, optional**

In a large bowl place the cake mix, flour, eggs, melted butter, honey, and orange zest. Mix with a wooden spoon until well blended and all dry ingredients are moistened. Chill, covered, at least 4 hours or overnight.

Preheat oven to 375° and spray cookie sheets with nonstick cooking spray. Position racks to upper and lower positions of oven.

Sprinkle a work surface with a thin layer of flour. Set out rolling pin, 2-inch cookie cutters, metal spatula, and cooling racks.

Remove the dough from the refrigerator and divide into fourths. Place one-fourth of the dough on floured surface (cover and return remaining dough to refrigerator). Flour the rolling pin and roll dough to ¼-inch thickness. Flour cookie cutters and cut-out shapes. Transfer dough to prepared cookie sheets with spatula. Re-roll any scraps, then repeat with remaining dough, rolling one fourth at a time.

Place one sheet on each oven rack. Bake 4 minutes. Rotate the sheets (place the sheet from the bottom rack on the top rack and the sheet from the top rack on the bottom rack. This ensures even baking). Bake 2–3 minutes longer.

Remove from oven and let cookies rest on sheets 1 minute. Transfer with metal spatula to racks and cool completely. Prepare Orange Icing; decorate cookies with icing and sprinkle with colored sugar, if desired.

Makes about 2 dozen 4-inch cookies.

Santa's Whiskers Cookies

These festive cookies are especially handy at holiday time—several batches can be made at once, refrigerated, then sliced and baked as needed.

1	18.25-ounce package white cake mix
½	cup shortening
⅓	cup butter, softened
1	large egg
1	cup red or green candied cherries (or combination of both), halved
1	tablespoon all-purpose flour
½	cup finely chopped pecans
2	cups sweetened flaked coconut

In a large bowl place the cake mix, shortening, butter, and egg. Blend with an electric mixer set on low speed for 1 minute (dough will be very thick). Scrape the dough off of the beaters.

In a small bowl combine cherries and tablespoon flour; toss to coat. Mix cherry mixture and pecans into dough by hand until combined.

Divide dough in half. Shape each dough piece into a 12 x 2-inch roll. Roll each in 1 cup coconut, pressing gently to adhere. Wrap each roll in plastic food wrap; refrigerate until firm (at least 4 hours).

Preheat oven to 350°. Position rack in center of oven. Cut rolls into ¼-inch slices with a sharp kitchen knife. Place 2 inches apart on ungreased cookie sheets.

Bake 7–8 minutes or until edges are lightly browned. Let stand on cookie sheets 1 minute. Transfer to wire rack and cool completely.

Makes about 5 dozen cookies.

FOUR

A Few Frostings and Finishes

Chocolate Drizzle or Dunk

Use this for drizzling onto cookies, or dunk cookies into it.

1 cup semisweet, milk chocolate, or white chocolate chips
1 tablespoon vegetable shortening

Melt chips and shortening in a small heavy saucepan over low heat, stirring often to avoid scorching. Makes about 1 cup melted chocolate, enough to drizzle over 4–5 dozen cookies, or spread onto one batch of biscotti.

To Use as a Chocolate Dip:

Dip a cookie or biscotti into the melted chocolate. Remove the excess chocolate by pulling the cookie across the edge of the pan.

To Use as a Chocolate Drizzle:

Place cookies on a wire rack over waxed paper. Dip a fork or knife into melted chocolate and let the first clumpy drip land back in the pan. Drizzle the chocolate over the edge of the pan onto the cookies. Place on wire rack. Let the cookies stand until the chocolate is set or refrigerate until chocolate is set.

Cookie Decorating Icing

1   16-ounce box powdered sugar
4   teaspoons powdered egg whites (not reconstituted)
⅓   cup water
1   tablespoon fresh lemon juice
1   teaspoon vanilla extract
    Food coloring paste, optional

In a large bowl beat together all ingredients except food coloring with an electric mixer set on medium speed until just blended, about 1 minute. Increase speed to high and continue to beat, scraping down side of bowl occasionally, until it holds stiff peaks, about 3 minutes in standing mixer or 4 to 5 minutes with a handheld mixer.

Beat in food coloring (if added color is desired). If you plan to spread (rather than pipe) icing on cookies, stir in more water, a few drops at a time, to thin to desired consistency.

Makes about 3 cups.

Chocolate Ganache

¾   cup heavy whipping cream
8   ounces semisweet baking chocolate, chopped

Heat the cream in a medium, heavy-bottomed saucepan set over low heat until cream is hot but not boiling; remove from heat.

Place chopped chocolate in medium bowl; pour hot cream over chocolate. Whisk mixture until chocolate is melted and mixture is glossy and smooth. Cool completely (several hours) before using as a frosting.

Makes about 2 cups.

Chocolate Sour Cream Frosting

¼ cup (½ stick) butter
1   cup semisweet chocolate chips
½   cup sour cream (not reduced fat)
1¼ cups sifted powdered sugar

In a medium saucepan set over low heat, combine butter and chocolate chips; cook and stir until melted and smooth. Remove from heat and cool 5 minutes; whisk in sour cream. Gradually add powdered sugar, whisking until blended, shiny and smooth.

Makes about 2 cups.

Chocolate Fudge Frosting

4   1-ounce squares unsweetened chocolate, coarsely chopped
6   tablespoons (¾ stick) butter, cut into pieces
3   cups powdered sugar, sifted, divided
2–3 tablespoons milk
1   teaspoon vanilla extract
pinch of salt

In a medium double boiler melt the chopped chocolate with the butter; cook and stir until melted and smooth. Remove from heat and cool 10 minutes.

In a medium bowl mix the melted chocolate, ½ cup powdered sugar, 1 tablespoon milk, vanilla extract, and pinch of salt with an electric mixer set on medium until blended. Add the remaining powdered sugar, ½ cup at a time, beating on medium speed until blended and smooth. Add a few more drops milk, if necessary, to make the frosting spreading consistency.

Makes about 2 cups.

Milk Chocolate Frosting

2 2-ounce squares unsweetened baking chocolate, coarsely chopped
½ cup (1 stick) butter, softened
¾ cup powdered sugar, sifted
½ cup heavy whipping cream

Fill a large skillet with 1 inch of water. Bring to a low simmer over medium-low heat. Place the chopped chocolate in large metal bowl; place the metal bowl in the skillet of water; stir chocolate until melted and smooth. Remove bowl from heat and cool 15 minutes.

Add the butter to bowl of melted chocolate. Beat with electric mixer set on medium until blended. Add the powdered sugar alternately with the cream, beating on medium until light and creamy. Add more sugar if too soft and more cream if too thick. Refrigerate 15 minutes.

Makes about 1⅔ cups.

Chocolate Cream Cheese Frosting

6 1-ounce squares semisweet, milk, or white chocolate, chopped
¼ cup heavy whipping cream
1 8-ounce package cream cheese, softened
2 cups powdered sugar, sifted

In double boiler melt the chopped chocolate with the heavy cream, mixing until melted and smooth. Remove from heat.

In a medium mixing bowl the beat cream cheese and powdered sugar with electric mixer set on medium until smooth. Slowly add the chocolate mixture, beating until incorporated and smooth. Cover and refrigerate at least 30 minutes (frosting will thicken up as the chocolate cools).

Makes about 2 cups.

Chocolate Marshmallow Frosting

2¼   cups powdered sugar, sifted
⅔   cup unsweetened cocoa powder
6   large marshmallows
¼   cup (½ stick) butter, cut into small pieces
5–6   tablespoons milk
1   teaspoon vanilla extract

In a large bowl combine the powdered sugar and cocoa powder. Set aside momentarily.

In a medium saucepan set over low heat, combine the marshmallows, butter, and milk, stirring constantly until melted and smooth, about 3 to 4 minutes. Remove the pan from the heat. Pour the marshmallow mixture over the sugar-cocoa mixture. Add the vanilla and stir until the frosting is smooth and satiny. Let stand 15–20 minutes to cool and thicken.

Makes about 1½ cups.

Fluffiest Chocolate Buttercream

2   1-ounce squares bittersweet or semisweet chocolate, coarsely chopped
½   of a 7-ounce jar marshmallow creme
¾   cup (1½ sticks) butter, softened and cut into chunks

In a medium double boiler set over simmering water, melt the chocolate, stirring until melted and smooth. Remove from heat and let cool, about 15–20 minutes.

In a medium bowl beat the marshmallow creme with an electric mixer on high until smooth. Gradually add the chunks of butter, mixing until incorporated, smooth and fluffy. Scrape bowl well and add the melted, cooled chocolate. Mix on high speed until incorporated and smooth. Use immediately.

Makes about 2 cups.

Chocolate-Raspberry Frosting

1   cup semisweet chocolate chips
⅔   cup sour cream
¼   cup seedless raspberry preserves, whisked to loosen
2   tablespoons light corn syrup
1   teaspoon vanilla extract
1½ tablespoons butter, softened

Stir chocolate in top of double boiler over simmering water until melted and smooth. Pour chocolate into large bowl. Cool to room temperature. Beat in the sour cream, preserves, corn syrup, and vanilla with an electric mixer set on medium, beating until mixture is fluffy, smooth and light in color, about 3 minutes. Beat in the butter.

Makes about 2 cups.

Quick Caramel Frosting

½   cup (1 stick) butter
1   cup packed dark brown sugar
¼   cup milk
2   cups powdered sugar, sifted
1   teaspoon vanilla extract

In a medium saucepan set over medium heat melt the butter with the brown sugar. Continue to cook and stir until the mixture comes to a boil. Add the milk; bring the mixture back to a boil. Remove the pan from the heat and stir in the powdered sugar and vanilla extract. Best if used right away, while still warm.

Makes about 2⅓ cups.

Cream Cheese Frosting

6   **ounces cream cheese, softened**
¼   **cup (½ stick) butter, softened**
1   **teaspoon vanilla extract**
2¼ **cups powdered sugar, sifted**

In a medium bowl beat the cream cheese, softened butter, and vanilla extract with an electric mixer set on medium speed until blended and smooth. Gradually add the powdered sugar, beating until incorporated and smooth.

Makes about 1¾ cups.

Sour Cream Frosting

¾   **cup powdered sugar**
1   **8-ounce package cream cheese, room temperature**
½   **cup sour cream**
1   **teaspoon fresh lemon juice**

In a medium bowl beat the powdered sugar, cream cheese, sour cream, and lemon juice with an electric mixer on high until well blended and smooth.

Makes about 1¾ cups.

Fruity Frosting

3   cups sifted powdered sugar
3   tablespoons butter, softened
⅔   cup preserves or jam, any variety

In a medium mixing bowl beat the powdered sugar, softened butter, and preserves at medium speed with electric mixer until smooth.

Makes about 1½ cups.

Fresh Citrus
(Lemon, Lime or Orange) Icing

3   cups sifted powdered sugar
2   teaspoons grated lemon, orange, or lime zest
5–6 tablespoons fresh lemon, orange, or lime juice

Place powdered sugar in medium bowl. Mix in zest and enough juice as needed to make icing just thin enough to drip off fork.

Makes about 1⅓ cups.

Browned Butter Icing

6   **tablespoons (¾ stick) butter (do not use margarine)**
3   **cups powdered sugar, sifted**
1½   **teaspoons vanilla extract**
1–2 tablespoons milk

Melt the butter in a medium saucepan set over medium heat until light brown in color (watch butter carefully—it can burn quickly). Remove from heat.

    Stir powdered sugar, vanilla extract, and 1 tablespoon milk into browned butter. Stir in just enough more milk to make frosting smooth and spreadable. Stir in more milk if mixture is too thick or more powdered sugar if mixture is too thin.

Makes about 1½ cups.

Peppermint Frosting

3   **cups powdered sugar, sifted**
⅓   **cup butter, softened**
¾   **teaspoon peppermint extract**
2–4 tablespoons milk
2   **drops green food coloring, optional**

In a medium bowl beat the powdered sugar, softened butter, and peppermint extract with an electric mixer set on low speed until blended and smooth. Beat in milk, 1 tablespoon at a time, until smooth and spreadable for frosting. For icing, add more milk until mixture is of drizzling consistency. Beat in green food coloring, if desired.

Makes about 1½ cups.

Orange–Cream Cheese Frosting

1   **8-ounce package cream cheese, softened**
3   **cups powdered sugar**
2   **tablespoons frozen orange juice concentrate, thawed**
1   **teaspoon grated orange zest**
1–2 drops yellow food color
1–2 drops red food color

In a small bowl mix the cream cheese, powdered sugar, orange juice concentrate, orange zest, yellow food color, and red food color until smooth and spreadable.

Makes about 1⅔ cups.

Peanut Butter Frosting

6   **tablespoons creamy-style peanut butter (not natural or old-fashioned style)**
¼   **cup (½ stick) butter, softened**
2   **cups powdered sugar, sifted**
3–4 tablespoons milk

In a medium mixing bowl beat the peanut butter and butter with an electric mixer set on medium until blended. Gradually add the powdered sugar alternately with the milk, beating on low speed until blended and smooth. Increase speed to medium and beat 1 minute longer, until light and creamy.

Makes about 1½ cups.

Maple Frosting

3   cups powdered sugar, sifted
2   3-ounce packages cream cheese, softened
2   tablespoons butter, softened
1   tablespoon maple-flavored extract

In a medium bowl beat the powdered sugar, softened cream cheese, butter, and maple flavoring until smooth.

Makes about 1¾ cups.

Vanilla Icing

4   cups powdered sugar, sifted
2–3 tablespoons whole milk
½   teaspoon vanilla extract

In a medium bowl combine the powdered sugar, 2 tablespoons milk, and vanilla extract. Stir until icing is well blended, smooth, and spreadable, adding more milk by teaspoonfuls if consistency is too thick.

Makes about 1½ cups.

Rum Icing

2 cups sifted powdered sugar
¼ cup (½ stick) butter, melted
2½ teaspoons rum-flavored extract, divided
2–3 tablespoons milk

In a small bowl combine the powdered sugar, butter, and rum flavoring. Add just enough milk to make icing of spreading consistency.

Makes about ¾ cup.

Brandy Icing

2 cups sifted powdered sugar
¼ cup (½ stick) butter, melted
2½ teaspoons brandy-flavored extract, divided
2–3 tablespoons milk

In a small bowl combine the powdered sugar, butter, and brandy flavoring. Add just enough milk to make icing of spreading consistency.

Makes about ¾ cup.

Glossary of Baking Terms

Beat: To combine ingredients vigorously with a spoon, fork, wire whisk, hand beater, or electric mixer until the ingredients are smooth and uniform.

Blend: To combine ingredients with a spoon, wire whisk, or rubber scraper until very smooth and uniform. A blender or food processor may also be used, depending on the job.

Boil: To heat a liquid until bubbles rise continuously and break on the surface and steam is given off. For a rolling boil, the bubbles form rapidly and will not stop forming even when the liquid is stirred.

Chop: To cut food into small pieces using a chef's knife, food processor, or blender.

Drain: To pour off extra liquid from a food, often with the use of a colander or strainer set over the sink. To reserve the drained liquid, place a bowl under the colander.

Drizzle: To slowly pour a liquid mixture, such as butter, chocolate, or glaze, in a very thin stream over a food.

Fold: To combine ingredients lightly while preventing loss of air by using two motions: Using a rubber spatula, first cut down vertically through the mixture. Next, slide the spatula across the bottom of the bowl and up the side, turning the mixture over. Repeat these motions after rotating the bowl one-fourth turn with each series of strokes.

Garnish: An edible decoration added to food or the act of adding such a decoration.

Grease: To rub the inside surface of a pan with solid shortening, using a pastry brush, waxed paper or paper towels, to prevent food from sticking during baking. Non-stick cooking spray may also be used; do not use butter or margarine (especially in a baked recipe) as either may burn and/or sticking may occur.

Grease and Flour: To rub the inside surface of a pan with solid shortening before dusting it with flour in order to prevent food from sticking during baking. After flouring the pan, turn it upside down and tap the bottom to remove excess flour.

Mix: To combine ingredients in any way that distributes them evenly, integrating the ingredients. This can be accomplished using a hand utensil or an electric mixer.

Pipe: A decorating technique that involves forcing frosting, icing, or chocolate from a pastry bag or parchment cone to form specific designs on a cookie.

Preheat: To turn the oven controls to the desired temperature, allowing the oven to heat thoroughly before adding food. Preheating takes about 10–15 minutes.

Set: To allow a food to become firm.

Soften: To allow cold food, such as butter, margarine, or cream cheese, to stand at room temperature until no longer hard. Generally this will take 30 to 60 minutes.

Stir: To combine ingredients with a circular or "figure 8" motion until they are of a uniform consistency.

Whip: To beat ingredients with a wire whisk, hand rotary beater, or electric mixer to add air and increase volume until ingredients are light and fluffy, such as with whipping cream or egg whites.

Zest: The perfume-y outermost layer of citrus fruit that contains the fruit's essential oils. Zest can be removed with a zester, a small handheld tool that separates the zest from the bitter white pith underneath, or with a grater, vegetable peeler, or sharp knife.

Index